Philippians
TO LIVE IS CHRIST

A Verse-By-Verse Bible Study
by

NANCY MCGUIRK

Advancing the Ministries of the Gospel
 AMG Publishers

God's Word to you is our highest calling.

CHATTANOOGA, TENNESSEE

Following God

PHILIPPIANS: TO LIVE AS CHRIST

© 2013 by Nancy McGuirk

ISBN: 978-0-89957-375-5
Third Printing, 2015

Cover design by Michael Largent
at InView Graphics, Chattanooga, TN (www.imagewright.net)

Editing by William Kruidenier, Barbara Scott, Christy Luellen, and Rick Steele

Typesetting and page layout by Jennifer Ross

This book is dedicated to the women of the:

Women's Community
Bible Study of Atlanta

I always experience the love of
Christ through you.

Acknowledgments

I've been blessed with gifted friends who have contributed meaningfully to preparing *To Live Is Christ*. Jill Turner read, critiqued, and proofread every lesson, with amazing attention to details. The Advisory Board of the Women's Community Bible Study of Atlanta prayed diligently for this project, offering feedback and encouragement since its inception. My husband and children, who gave love and support throughout the process, were my greatest cheerleaders. William Kruidenier applied his excellent editorial skills to each page. And Rick Steele, Barbara Scott, Jennifer Ross, and the wonderful team at AMG Publishers, oversaw this project with grace and good cheer every step of the way.

Most of all, I gladly and gratefully acknowledge the triune God of Scripture: the Father who loves me, the Son who saves me, and the Spirit who sanctifies me. To them be all the glory!

Nancy McGuirk

About the Author

Nancy Davis McGuirk is the founder and lead teacher for Women's Community Bible Study in Atlanta, Georgia (wcbsonline.org). WCBS impacts nearly 500 women who meet weekly to study, pray, and grow in Christ. Since 1990, Nancy's ministry of evangelism, teaching, writing, and discipleship has impacted women in Atlanta and beyond. Satellite groups in other cities receive Nancy's ministry via printed, video, and audio media.

Nancy has authored a number of study materials including *My New Life in Christ*, an eight-week curriculum based on the foundational principles of the Christian faith, and *Rest Assured*, a 90-day devotional that offers scriptural teachings on spiritual rest. Nancy was a featured columnist on Christianity.com and is a popular speaker for churches, women's groups, and conference venues such as The Billy Graham Training Center at The Cove.

Nancy and her husband, Terry, are parents to four grown children and grandparents to a growing group of grandchildren.

Visit Nancy's web site at nancymcguirk.com.

About the Following God Series

Three authors and fellow ministers, Wayne Barber, Eddie Rasnake, and Rick Shepherd, teamed up in 1998 to write a character-based Bible study for AMG Publishers. Their collaboration developed into the title, *Life Principles from the Old Testament*. Since 1998 these same authors and AMG Publishers have produced six more **character-based** studies—each consisting of twelve lessons geared around a five-day study of a particular Bible personality. In 2001, AMG Publishers launched a series of topical studies called the **Following God™ Discipleship Series**. Soon after, books were released in the Following God™ **Christian Living Series,** which is also topical in nature. Though new studies and authors are being introduced, the interactive study format that readers have come to love remains constant with each new Following God™ release. As new titles and categories are being planned, our focus remains the same: to provide excellent Bible study materials that point people to God's Word in ways that allow them to apply truths to their own lives. More information on this groundbreaking series can be found on the following web page:

www.amgpublishers.com

Table of Contents

INTRODUCTION

Imagine I placed before you an ancient treasure chest and told you it contained riches that could change your life forever. The gems in this chest would provide for a life of joy regardless of circumstances and grant triumph in the midst of tragedy. Would you be eager to open such a treasure chest? You are about to do just that, for the treasure chest is none other than the Apostle Paul's letter to the Philippians. For generations, his words have been the foundation for a life of contentment and joy to all who have embraced them.

Can you imagine how the Philippians must have felt when they first unrolled the scroll sent by their spiritual father, Paul, and listened to his messenger read to them aloud? The Philippian Christians were facing persecution, poverty, and heresy at that time, and they desperately needed hope—a lifeline to grasp. Today we're surrounded by terrorism, materialism, spiritual darkness, divorce, disease, recession, and war. Like the Philippians, we need to hear the encouraging words of Paul, words that will lead us to rise above the circumstances that try to steal our joy.

The most amazing aspect of Paul's perspective on his life is that he wrote his "epistle of joy" to the Philippians while sitting in a Roman jail. From his vantage point, his earthly future was uncertain. While writing in those circumstances, how could he encourage the Philippians to be joyful? What was his motivation? His perspective? What did Paul know that could allow us to maintain joy when faced with our own uncertain futures?

Paul's joy was not derived from prosperity and success. He possessed none of the things the average Christian depends on today to help cope with difficult times, such as insurance, savings accounts, counselors, or friends, who are a phone call away. Even when not in jail, Paul's life was still filled with hardship and pressure. It wasn't the absence of hardship that allowed Paul to retain his joy. Instead, he knew the secret to being joyful *in* difficult times. We all want to experience Paul's joy, but none of us wants to endure the hardship Paul experienced from which his joy arose. The reality is that our deepest joy comes from discovering the sufficiency of Christ's strength when our strength is depleted. And that is why we need to learn Paul's secrets of contentment and joy. The question is not whether we will experience difficult circumstances, but how will we respond to them. Everyone faces trials. If we are not currently in, or coming out of, a rough patch, we will undoubtedly come upon one soon.

Paul's secret of contentment is found in his well-known words, "to live is Christ" (Philippians 1:21). The goal of this Bible study, and my heartfelt prayer, is that God will reveal to us through this powerful little book how to rise above the circumstances of life, experience joy amidst adversity, and live with Christ at the center of our lives.

How about those for priceless principles? Now let's open up this treasure chest and dig in!

BACKGROUND

THE APOSTLE PAUL

Paul of Tarsus (the Apostle Paul) was a Jew called by Christ to be the "Apostle to the Gentiles" (Acts 9:15; Acts 22:21; Acts 26:17–18; Romans 11:13; Galatians 2:8). *Apostolos* is a Greek word that means "a person sent; a messenger." Paul was a messenger for Christ commissioned to spread the Gospel to the Gentiles—the non-Jewish population of the world.

Paul grew up in the Mediterranean city of Tarsus in present-day Turkey, well-known for its intellectual environment. Named Saul from birth, Paul was probably born around the same time as Jesus as a descendant of the tribe of Benjamin, and he became a well-educated Pharisee and a strict follower of the law (Philippians 3:4–6). According to his own testimony, Paul (prior to his conversion to Christ) had "persecuted the church of God" (Acts 9:1–2; 1 Corinthians 15:9; Galatians 1:13). He also supported and witnessed the death of the first martyr, Stephen, who was stoned to death (Acts 7:54—8:1).

Around 35 AD, Paul experienced a personal, life-changing revelation on the road to Damascus, where he was confronted in a vision by the resurrected Jesus. After suffering blindness for three days, the Christians in the church at Damascus (Acts 9:1–19) ministered to him. Several years later he was presented to the leaders of the church in Jerusalem and accepted by them but was forced to return to his hometown of Tarsus for protection from the Jews in Jerusalem (Acts 9:23–30).

Many years later, Barnabas asked Paul to leave Tarsus and help him with the growing church in Antioch (Acts 11:19–26). That church became the base for Paul's three missionary journeys of evangelism and church planting throughout the Mediterranean world. A fourth journey was undertaken after release from his first imprisonment in Rome. Thirteen New Testament epistles are attributed to Paul.

Paul was imprisoned in Rome for a second time and died as a martyr for Christ around A.D. 67–68.

Paul's influence on Christianity has been far greater than any other New Testament writer. In the Epistle of St. Clement, who was the fourth Bishop of Rome about 90 A.D., Clement gives this report about Paul's dedication to the spreading of the Gospel:

> *"By reason of jealousy and strife Paul, by example, pointed out the prize of patient endurance. After that he had been seven times in bonds, had been driven in exile, had been stoned, had preached in the east and the west, he won the noble renown which was the reward for his faith, having taught righteousness unto the whole world and having reached the farthest bounds of the west; and when he had borne his testimony before the rulers, so he departed from the world unto the holy place, having been found a notable pattern of patient endurance."*

THE CITY OF PHILIPPI

Philippi was originally known as Krenides, "The Little Fountains," because of the numerous nearby springs. It was located in the Roman province of

Macedonia, which we know as modern-day Greece, and founded around 360 B.C. by King Phillip II, after whom it was named. Phillip was the father of Alexander the Great. After the Romans defeated the Greeks in 168 B.C., Philippi became part of the Roman Empire. At the time of Paul, the citizens of Philippi were mostly Roman, though there were some Greeks and a few Jews. Luke described Philippi as "the leading city of that district of Macedonia" (Acts 16:12), which speaks to Paul's strategy of evangelizing in important cities. Philippi was the first "European" city to hear the Gospel as far as we know (Acts 16:11–12).

THE CHURCH AT PHILIPPI

While on his second missionary journey, Paul founded the church in Philippi (Acts 16). The journey began as a difficult one. Barnabas, Paul's companion on the first missionary journey, wanted to take along his (Barnabas's) cousin Mark. But Paul was adamantly opposed, since Mark had deserted them on the previous trip. So Paul and Barnabas split (Acts 15:36–41), with Paul taking Silas instead.
After spreading the Gospel in Asia Minor (modern-day Turkey) . . .

> *"Paul and his companions traveled throughout the region of Phyrgia and Galatia, having been kept by the Holy Spirit from preaching the word in the province of Asia. When they came to the border of Mysia, they tried to enter Bithynia, but the Spirit of Jesus would not allow them to. So they passed by Mysia and went down to Troas" (Acts 16:6-8).*

At Troas, "During the night, Paul had a vision of a man of Macedonia standing and begging [Paul], 'Come over to Macedonia and help us'" (Acts 16:9). Paul concluded that God was directing them to take the Gospel to Macedonia, so he and his companions sailed immediately across the Aegean Sea to Macedonia, arriving at the seaport of Neapolis (Acts 16:11). Paul, Silas, Timothy, and Luke pressed on to the city of Philippi to begin work.

Paul's custom was to preach first in the local Jewish synagogue, but it appears there was not one in Philippi. Going outside the city gate, they encountered a group of women who had gathered on the banks of a river to pray, and Paul joined them. There he met Lydia, a successful merchant, whose business was trading purple cloth for which her hometown of Thyatira was famous. She listened to Paul's message and was converted along with her whole household. They were the first European Christians. Lydia was not Jewish but was a "worshiper of God" (Acts 16:14)–a Gentile who participated in Jewish worship without converting to Judaism. Her house became the center of missionary activity in Philippi.

Shortly thereafter, Paul ran into trouble. After casting a demon out of a fortune–telling slave girl, the girl lost her ability to predict the future. This outraged her owners, who realized they would lose a great deal of money because of this. So they had Paul and Silas thrown into jail.

That night, while the two of them were singing hymns and praying, an earthquake shook the jail open. The jailer saw the open door and, fearing that all his prisoners had fled and he would be severely punished, was about to commit suicide. But Paul stopped him and reported that all the prisoners were still there. With great emotion, the Philippian jailer asked Paul and Silas how he might be saved, and he and his household became Christians (Acts 16:30–34).

The next day, when it was discovered that Paul and Silas were Roman citizens, they were released without harm. But they were asked to leave the city. Though Paul and Silas left Philippi, they left behind the first "European" church. There is some evidence that Luke stayed behind to guide the young church. The Philippian church always had a special place in Paul's heart—so much so that, years later, in his epistle, he called them his "joy and crown" (Philippians 4:1).

THE LETTER TO THE CHURCH AT PHILIPPI

There was unanimous agreement in the early church that the Apostle Paul was the author of the letter to the Philippians, but the place of its writing is less sure. It was obvious Paul wrote from jail (Philippians 1:12–17), but he was imprisoned more than once. The majority of the evidence favors Paul writing to the Philippians from his first, two-year, imprisonment in Rome (Acts 28:14–31; Philippians 4:22) in "Caesar's household" around 61 A.D., during which time he wrote all of the "Prison Epistles": Ephesians, Philippians, Colossians, and Philemon.

This imprisonment was more of a house arrest, during which Paul was free to receive visitors and carry on correspondence and teaching. Paul probably dictated all his letters to a "secretary," signing them with his own hand at the end (1 Corinthians 16:21; Galatians 6:11; Colossians 4:18; 2 Thessalonians 3:17). But he appears to have written Philemon himself (Philemon 19). All of Paul's letters were written to address specific needs in specific churches, although even in the first century they were recognized as authoritative for all the churches (2 Peter 3:15–16).

During Paul's imprisonment, Epaphroditus, an old friend from Philippi, arrived bearing a gift from the church (Philippians 4:10–20). Paul then sent a letter back to the Philippians thanking them for their gift and for all they meant to him, which later became our New Testament book of Philippians. Paul also informed them he hoped to send Timothy to see them soon (Philippians 2:19) and he would come when he was released from prison. He also warned them of the danger they faced from certain troublemakers who sought to undermine their doctrine and morals and the danger they faced if they did not remain unified.

Philippians is one of the most personal of all of Paul's letters. He is writing to trusted friends and followers in the faith. In this letter, he demonstrates a unique informality, a tenderness of heart, and a freedom of expression. It is considered one of the loveliest letters ever written by Paul and has been called by two titles: "The Epistle of Excellent Things" and "The Epistle of Joy." Paul told his friends, even while writing "in chains," to rejoice in the one truth that "to live is Christ."

HOW TO USE THIS STUDY

To Live is Christ is an eight-week, verse-by-verse Bible study. In the front of this book you will find background information on the apostle Paul and his journeys: biographical information plus a map of his travels along with descriptions of the people he met and significant events along the way.

The Bible study itself covers the entire book of Philippians with five daily units for each week—a total of 40 lessons. Each daily unit has a commentary for the verses from Philippians for that day, as well as questions for both group study and personal reflection. There is also a prayer to stimulate your response to God based on what you learned that day. In the sidebars you will find quotes from famous theologians, word studies, and theological facts to enhance your study. Day five's lesson in each week is a review of the lessons from days one through four, and there are questions to help you summarize what you have learned for that week.

While the purpose of each lesson is to understand what Paul wrote to the Philippians, the larger goal is to understand how the timeless principles of Scripture can impact your life. Paul wanted the Philippians to live with joy and contentment—and God wants the same for you.

PREPARATION FOR THIS STUDY

The ultimate teacher and expositor of the Word of God is the Holy Spirit, the One who inspired its writing. Only He can open a person's spiritual heart and eyes to grasp the present and eternal implications of the truth of Scripture. Therefore, it is imperative for the reader of Scripture to be submitted to the ministry of the Spirit so as not to hinder His illuminating work. When a person places his or her faith in Jesus Christ as Lord and Savior, the Holy Spirit comes to dwell in that person's life. If you have never placed your faith in Christ, or if you are not sure of your relationship with Him, consider bowing your heart before God and praying a prayer like the following before beginning the study of Philippians:

 Dear God, I want to know You, and I want to understand Your Word. Before beginning to study Philippians, I affirm my desire to belong to You through faith in Jesus Christ as my Lord and Savior. Please forgive my sins and grant that I might be born again as a citizen of Your heavenly eternal kingdom. Please fill me with Your Holy Spirit in order that I may know and understand Your Word. Thank You for Your promise to love me and guide me by the ministry of the Spirit. I pray this prayer in the name of Christ my Lord. Amen.

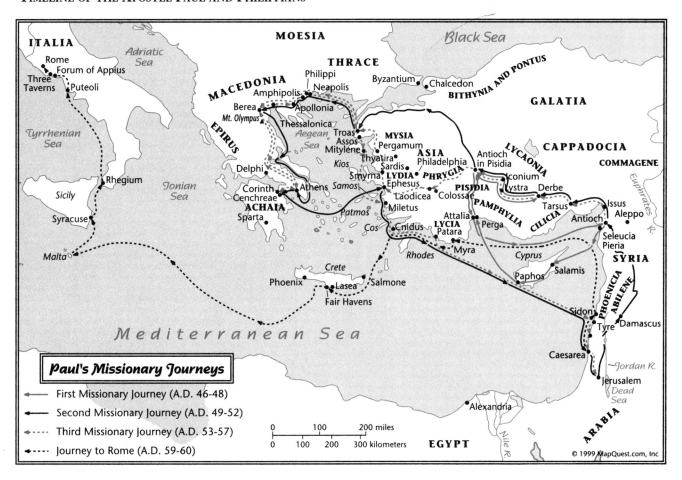

Birth (reared in Tarsus)	8 A.D.
Conversion on the road to Damascus	3–35
Spends three years in Arabia	35–37
First visit to Jerusalem	37
First missionary journey	46–49
Jerusalem Conference	49–50
Second missionary journey (Paul visited Philippi after receiving a vision from a man in Macedonia)	51–52
Third missionary journey	53–58
Paul arrested and imprisoned in Rome	60
Paul writes Philippians during two-year imprisonment in Rome	60–62
Paul was released, later rearrested, imprisoned, and martyred in Rome	67

* all dates are approximate

Acts 16:6-40

LESSON OVERVIEW
EVANGELISM

He was determined. Nothing would stop him.

In spite of walking miles of dusty roads, enduring hardships, beatings, imprisonments, sleepless nights, hunger, dishonor, rejection, poverty, flogging, stoning, and shipwreck, he would never give up. Why?

Paul was on a mission that was too important. It changed his life completely and would change the lives of all who heard and believed his message.

What was Paul thinking as he walked those roads from town to town? Did he feel guilt for standing with the crowd in Jerusalem as Stephen was stoned to death? Did he regret his misguided passion to annihilate all Christians who belonged to this new cult called "the Way"? Was he embarrassed by his own pride and religiosity? He must have been so overwhelmed with the love and mercy of Christ that his gratitude overcame that guilt.

On the road to Damascus, Paul was blinded—literally and figuratively. But now he could see. He could experience the grace, love, compassion, and mercy that flowed from his Savior, the One whom he had persecuted. That is the mercy of Jesus. And Paul had to share that mercy. So he and his companions made missionary trips to spread the Gospel. On their second trip they made their way to Philippi. Little did this community know that many lives were going to change drastically.

But the grace of Jesus did not end with the passing of the apostles. It has continued for generations. Jesus has continued to send out messengers time and time again guided by the Holy Spirit with the same results—transformed lives. For when God's Word goes out, it does not return void.

Once your heart is truly changed, you will be compelled to get out the message too. The good news that Christ loves us, died for us, has a plan for our lives, and wants us to enter eternity when we die, is just too good not to share.

Acts 16:6-40

DAY ONE

Did You Know?

JERUSALEM COUNCIL

Part of the reason for Paul's second missionary journey was to report to the churches in Asia Minor about the decisions reached by the leaders in Jerusalem concerning Christians' responsibility to Jewish ceremonial laws and traditions. Known as the Jerusalem Council, this meeting was the first gathering of Christian leaders in church history to forge doctrinal and practical guidelines for the Christian community (see Acts 15:1–35).

GUIDED TOWARD PHILIPPI (ACTS 16:6)

Some men are known for never asking for directions, and my husband is one of them. But it's not for the reason you might think. It's just that he really does have an amazing sense of direction. Recently, he was driving us through the mountains of Virginia to visit our daughter, and I was convinced he was off course. Nothing looked familiar. He then delighted in showing me that he was using a shortcut to our destination and, as it turned out, a more scenic route as well.

Sometimes the way I acted toward my husband on that trip is like how we lack faith in God. We get confused by circumstances and surroundings and think we are on the wrong path, only to discover later that God was leading us perfectly all the time.

Paul's letter to the Philippians came to be written because God changed Paul's direction. Paul didn't set out for Philippi, but he also didn't end up there by accident. He set out following God's will for his life and, some time and events later, there he was—in Philippi. God was faithful to get Paul and his companions where they needed to be.

Our lives are like that. We often aren't sure where we're going in terms of the details. However, our goals are to be obedient and faithful to what we do know when it comes to following Christ. When we look back, we can see how God directed our paths in ways we couldn't have planned or expected. That's what happened to Paul and his companions, and it's often what happens to us.

PERMISSION GRANTED TO PREACH

Paul and his companions traveled throughout the region of Phrygia and Galatia. (Acts 16:6a)

Before we get to what happened with Paul and Barnabas, let's get our footing in the geography of this passage. Paul and Barnabas are about to set out on what we now call their "second missionary journey." This is the trip that God directed and one they probably never imagined they were about to embark on.

From what city and church did Paul and Barnabas set out on their second missionary journey? What was their purpose in going (Acts 15:35–36)?

_____

_____

_____

There were two cities named Antioch in the Mediterranean region: one in Syria, north of the land of Israel (Syrian Antioch) and another in Asia Minor (Pisidian Antioch in modern Turkey). In Syrian Antioch, a strong church made up of Jewish-Christian refugees from Jerusalem developed. Paul and Silas left Syrian Antioch with a plan to visit the churches in Asia Minor, which they had started or visited on Paul's first missionary trip. On the map in the front of this book, locate Antioch in Syria. Then look toward the western coast of Asia Minor, across the Aegean Sea, and locate Philippi in ancient Macedonia. When Paul and Silas left Antioch, they had not planned to cross the Aegean Sea into Philippi in present-day Europe. Their plans were to visit churches in Asia Minor (Acts 15:36). But the itinerary God had in mind for this pair was quite different.

📖 From Acts 26:15–18, what do you learn about Paul's understanding of God's calling and plan for his life?

_____

_____

_____

Every Christian has a general calling from God that is the same for every follower of Jesus. What parts of that calling are revealed in the following verses?

📖 Matthew 22:37–40

_____

_____

📖 Matthew 28:19–20

_____

_____

📖 Romans 12:1–2

_____

_____

📖 But what does Psalm 139:16 and Romans 12:3–6a suggest about God having a specific calling for your life that is different from his plan for others?

_____

_____

_____

Compare the way you follow God's general calling for your life as a Christian to Paul and Silas traveling throughout Asia Minor. Paul and Silas had a geographic boundary within which they could make choices.

> **"Service to God through service to mankind is the only motivation acceptable to God for diligence and hard work in our vocational calling."**
> **Jerry Bridges**

Did You Know?
ASIA MINOR/TURKEY

The region of Syria, home of Paul's "sending" church at Antioch, is still called Syria today—a nation by the same name as in the first century. But the region of Asia Minor—a collection of provinces which were overseen by Rome—is today the modern nation of Turkey. On the Western edge of Turkey is modern Istanbul, formerly named Constantinople (fourth century), the capital of the Eastern branch of the Roman Empire and eventually the base of the Eastern Orthodox Church after it split from the Roman Catholic church in the 11th century.

Put Yourself in Their Shoes

TIMOTHY

Timothy, a well-known figure in the New Testament, comes on the scene in Acts 16:1–3. After Paul and Barnabas parted ways (Acts 15:37–40), Paul joined with Silas and journeyed to Lystra where they met a young Christian named Timothy who was well spoken of by the church at Lystra. Paul recruited Timothy to travel with Silas and him as they journeyed through Asia Minor. Timothy became one of Paul's most valued co-laborers in the Gospel.

APPLY Geographic or otherwise, we all have boundaries that constrain our choices. What boundaries confine or compel your choices and decisions as a Christian?

_____

_____

_____

_____

_____

What explanation does Proverbs 16:9 provide for how we can exercise freedom within God's boundaries as we plan and act in life?

_____

_____

_____

The Christian life is to be lived as a partnership with Jesus Christ (Mark 16:20). He is our Lord, and we are His servants. But as the parable in Matthew 25:14–30 illustrates, masters give their servants a great deal of latitude when it comes to fulfilling their responsibilities. And so God gives us great breadth and freedom to serve Him in the ways that we have prayerfully and biblically considered. God is perfectly capable of stepping into our plans and closing a door in order to sharpen our focus and head us in another way. If God occasionally said "No," then "Yes," to the Apostle Paul, we shouldn't be surprised when He does the same with us.

PERMISSION DENIED TO PREACH

> *. . . having been kept by the Holy Spirit from preaching the word in the province of Asia. (Acts 16:6b)*

One of the biggest challenges of the Christian life is discerning God's guidance in our lives. There are a number of variables at work in this process:

1. Our innate human sense of curiosity: sometimes we want to *know* God's will more than we want to *do* it.
2. Our desire to please the Lord: sometimes we feel like saying, "Just tell me what you want, Lord, and I'll do it!"
3. Our process of transitioning from spiritual infancy to adulthood: sometimes it's easier to remain in infancy to be told what to do than it is to accept the responsibility for learning to make choices based on wisdom from God.
4. Our need to walk by faith, not by sight: sometimes we're hesitant to trust the guidance we have received and step out in faith.

Sometimes Christians mistakenly think that God purposely hides His will from us just for the pleasure of correcting us when we do the wrong thing—like an unloving parent. Nothing could be further from the truth. Just because God doesn't reveal His will immediately and clearly every time we want to know it doesn't mean He is toying with us. The Bible is clear about this: God is good and loving, a benevolent Father who is continually moving us forward in the process of becoming like Jesus Christ (Romans 8:29). But He does that on His timetable and according to His will.

Even Paul sometimes only knew the big picture of God's calling. God revealed the calling (take the Gospel to the Gentiles) but left a lot of the strategy to unfold along the way. Paul set out in faith, trusting God would guide him in whatever way he needed. And we should do the same.

Apparently, when Paul and his companions left Syrian Antioch and entered Asia Minor, they reached the central region (perhaps at Pisidian Antioch) and decided to head southwest into the region of Asia, but they were "kept by the Holy Spirit" from executing that strategy. We are not told how the Spirit constrained them—only that He did.

APPLY What means might God use in a Christian's life today to say "no" and move that person in a different direction? Describe a time when God said "no" to you, the means He used, and how you responded:

_____

_____

_____

_____

_____

Responding to Scripture

What is the central idea of Acts 16:6?

_____

_____

_____

Responding to Life

How can you apply this idea to your life? Can you see God directing you toward or away from a certain destination now? Or has He done so in the past?

_____

_____

_____

Responding to God

 Heavenly Father, thank You for allowing me to partner with Jesus Christ in spreading the reality of Your kingdom and His Gospel throughout the earth. I pray for wisdom to make choices that honor You. And I pray for grace to allow You to direct my path in the way that You see fit. May Your will be done in my life whether You say no or yes to me. Let it, to me, make no difference where You send me, but only that I follow You always. In Christ's name I pray. Amen.

GETTING TO MACEDONIA (ACTS 16:7-10)

Y ou've heard the expression, "The best laid plans of mice and men . . . ." It's often repeated, with a sigh of resignation, when the plans we have made are changed in an unforeseen way. What we don't often see, except with the advantage of hindsight, is that the change God allowed was for the better.

Take England's William Wilberforce, for example. In spite of being weak and sickly as a youth, his plan was to become prime minister of his country. But a "chance" reading of Philip Doddridge's book, *The Rise and Progress of Religion in the Soul*, led to his conversion to Christ. His conversion was genuine as he spoke out about the immorality and apathy found in the British Parliament. He became known as "the conscience of Parliament," especially concerning England's participation in the African slave trade. Though the slave trade contributed significantly to England's national economy, Wilberforce knew God was opposed to it and it had to be stopped.

For twenty years, Wilberforce was the voice for abolishing England's slave trade. His tireless work led to failing health, forcing him to retire from Parliament. Seven years later, just three days before his death, news reached Wilberforce that the Slavery Abolition Act would be approved by Parliament.

William Wilberforce never became prime minister of England, but the change in his life's direction resulted in an impact on the world far greater than he had ever planned.[1]

The Apostle Paul's life was radically changed too. A fire-breathing hater of Christians, he sought and received orders to kill believers in Jesus and was unrelenting in his pursuit of Christians until one day God changed his path. Paul then traveled far and wide to spread the message of the One who had knocked him down and blinded him on the road to Damascus, who had restored his sight and given him a new life and purpose.

When God prevented Paul from entering Bithynia, it may have been as simple as the brief Scripture makes it sound. Because God had so radically changed Paul's plans once, it is unlikely a minor change of geographical plans was going to set him back.

Sometimes the road to our destination is curvy and bumpy. The larger the task, the less straight the road seems to be. Our task is to let God lay out the road in His way, to watch for the signposts, and to follow the road faithfully until we arrive at the destination and accomplish His purpose, whether large or small in our sight. Every calling is critical in God's plan.

Paul and his companions didn't know it, but God was sending them into modern-day Europe—ancient Macedonia—to preach the Gospel of Christ. Their road was circuitous, but they were faithful. And when God finally revealed their destination, they responded with immediate obedience.

OBSTACLES ON THE WAY

When they came to the border of Mysia, they tried to enter Bithynia, but the

Doctrine
THE SPIRIT OF JESUS

The Holy Spirit is called "the Spirit of Jesus" only in Acts 16:7 and Philippians 1:19 (*"the Spirit of Jesus Christ"*). There is clear scriptural evidence that the Spirit was sent to indwell Christians by Jesus (John 15:26), beginning at Pentecost (Acts 2:33). Therefore, the "Spirit of Jesus" can also be understood as the "Spirit from, or given by, Jesus."

Spirit of Jesus would not allow them to. So they passed by Mysia and went down to Troas. (Acts 16:7–8)

Paul and his companions might have felt a bit like steel balls in a pinball machine, bouncing from place to place. It was as if they entered a wide-mouth funnel when they entered Asia Minor. The further they went, the narrower the funnel became until they arrived just where God wanted them: Troas.

📖 Scripture does not say, but what do you imagine Paul and his companions were doing as they traveled? Were these side trips unfruitful? Wasted time and effort? How do we know that no "side trip" in our life is ever wasted (Genesis 50:20; Exodus 13:17–18; Romans 8:28)?

_____

_____

_____

_____

📖 We don't know what "the Spirit of Jesus" (the Holy Spirit) did to block Paul's entrance into Bithynia. God used supernatural means at times to speak to the apostles (Acts 16:9; Acts 21:10–11; Acts 23:11), but at other times, circumstances such as open doors or closed doors no doubt came into play. Why is it important to pay attention to everything God allows to enter your life? Based on verses like Matthew 10:29–30, how aware of details is God?

_____

_____

_____

_____

📖 Discernment is the ability to exhibit sound insight and judgment; to take in information and reach wise conclusions. It is also a key theme in the book of Proverbs. (See Proverbs 1:5; Proverbs 3:21; Proverbs 10:13; and Proverbs 15:14). Why is spiritual discernment so important in following God's leading?

_____

_____

_____

📖 When you are uncertain about a circumstance or situation when following God, what should you do (Proverbs 2:3–5)? What will God do (Proverbs 2:6)?

_____

_____

_____

_____

"Wisdom in ruling is justice; wisdom in speech is discretion; wisdom in conduct is prudence, wisdom in evaluation is discernment."

George Seevers

OBEDIENCE TO THE WAY

During the night Paul had a vision of a man of Macedonia standing and begging him, "Come over to Macedonia and help us." After Paul had seen the vision, we got ready at once to leave for Macedonia, concluding that God had called us to preach the gospel to them. (Acts 16:9–10)

In the first century, Christianity was often referred to as "The Way" (Acts 9:2), perhaps based on Jesus referring to himself as "the way and the truth and the life" in John 14:6. The Christian life is a journey lived by following "The Way" of Christ and the leading of the Holy Spirit. Paul's ultimate goal in life was to live in obedience to that Way, and ours should be too (Philippians 3:7–15).

📖 After arriving in Troas, what happened to Paul "during the night" as he slept (Acts 16:9)?

_____

_____

_____

📖 Given the spiritual nature of Paul's mission, what do you think "Come over to Macedonia and help us" meant (Acts 16:9–10b)?

_____

_____

_____

Why was Paul's response to the vision a good illustration of this axiom: "Delayed obedience is disobedience?" Why do you think Paul and his companions didn't wait until morning to begin making their way to Macedonia?

_____

_____

Responding to Scripture

State in your own words the main idea or theme of Acts 16:7–10.

_____

_____

_____

_____

Responding to Life

What impact on your life could this example from the life of Paul and his companions have?

_____

_____

_____

_____

"Faith and obedience are bound up in the same bundle. He that obeys God, trusts God; and he that trusts God, obeys God."

C. H. Spurgeon

Heavenly Father, thank You for caring about the details of my life and for using whatever is necessary to guide me in "The Way" of following Jesus day-by-day. I call out to You for wisdom and discernment to see the signposts You use to direct my way. Help me to obey immediately when Your way becomes clear to me. In Christ's name, I pray. Amen.

GATEWAY TO CONVERSIONS (ACTS 16:11–15)

Think of all the groups and causes you have joined in your lifetime: clubs, churches, civic groups, humanitarian causes, social groups. Joining requires an evaluation and a decision, a mental and an emotional process. But when we join ourselves to Christ and become His followers, something besides a mental and emotional component is needed. God has to open our hearts to see our need for Christ and the truth that He is Lord and Savior. This is a supernatural process.

When Paul and his companions arrived in Philippi, they met a moral, upstanding, businesswoman named Lydia. She was a worshiper of God, but not of Jesus. Through Paul, God opened her heart to respond to the good news about Christ, and she became a Christian. What happened to Lydia is what happens to anyone who places his or her faith in Christ: God opens the eyes of the heart.

THE FIRST CONVERT

> From Troas we put out to sea and sailed straight for Samothrace, and the next day on to Neapolis. From there we traveled to Philippi, a Roman colony and the leading city of that district of Macedonia. And we stayed there several days. On the Sabbath we went outside the city gate to the river, where we expected to find a place of prayer. We sat down and began to speak to the women who had gathered there. One of those listening was a woman named Lydia, a dealer in purple cloth from the city of Thyatira, who was a worshiper of God. The Lord opened her heart to respond to Paul's message. (Acts 16:11–14)

Paul, Silas, Timothy, and Luke set sail from the port city of Troas and landed in Macedonia. They traveled inland a few miles to Philippi, "the leading city of that district of Macedonia." Since there weren't enough Jews in Philippi to form a synagogue, Jews and other "God-fearers" met for prayer on the banks of a river. Paul encountered this group, apparently all women, on his first Sabbath in Philippi and shared the Gospel with them. God opened Lydia's heart to believe in Christ.

📖 Fill in what you learn about Lydia from Acts 16:14:

- Her vocation: _____

- Her hometown: _____

- Her perspective toward God:_____

> "The Bible recognizes no faith that does not lead to obedience, nor does it recognize any obedience that does not spring from faith. The two are opposite sides of the same coin."
>
> **A. W. Tozer**

 Did You Know?

SYNAGOGUES

When the Old Testament Jews were driven into exile in Assyria and Babylon and no longer had access to the temple in Jerusalem for worship, they gathered in synagogues ("place of assembly") for worship and Scripture reading. Tradition required the presence of a minimum of 10 Jewish men in order to constitute a synagogue. By the time of Christ and the apostles, synagogues existed throughout the Mediterranean world. Synagogues were often located near running water, which was used for ritual cleansings.

Lydia was a Gentile seeker—a person who believed in God and sought after Him the best way she knew how, probably following the customs of Jews who worshipped God. But the full revelation of God's work through Jesus Christ had not reached Philippi. When Lydia heard the Gospel message, God gave her faith, by grace, to believe (Ephesians 2:8–9). What happened to Lydia was the same thing that happened to two downcast followers of Christ following the crucifixion (Luke 24:45).

📖 Meditate on Luke 24:25, Ephesians 2:1, 5, and Romans 3:10–18 and explain why God has to intervene and give man the ability to believe.

_____

_____

_____

I had my own "heart-opening" experience years ago. I was an upstanding, church-going, God-worshipping, young wife and mother who thought I had done everything right when it came to knowing God. But God used the words of a Bible teacher to open my heart to see I lacked a personal relationship with Him through Christ. My intelligence, respectability, and piety weren't enough. I needed the forgiveness of my sins and the gift of the Holy Spirit in my life, both of which come only through faith in Christ.

On the day my heart was opened, I was converted from faith in Nancy and God to faith in God through Christ alone. For the first time I felt loved for who I was, faults and all. I knew in my heart I had much to learn, but also that God had a plan for my life. I was now in a relationship with my Creator who was there to listen to my prayers and concerns and who would communicate His desire for my life through His Word. Amazing.

APPLY If your heart has been opened to see your need for Christ, describe how that happened and the changes that resulted.

_____

_____

_____

THE FIRST CHURCH

When she and the members of her household were baptized, she invited us to her home. "If you consider me a believer in the Lord," she said, "come and stay at my house." And she persuaded us. (Acts 16:15)

As far as we know, Lydia was the first convert to Christ in Philippi and possibly in all of modern-day Europe as a result of the Apostle Paul's ministry. She did what every new convert to Christ should do after believing: she and her household, who also believed, were baptized.

📖 What was the basis for Paul's urging new converts to be baptized upon their profession of faith (Matthew 28:19–20; Acts 16:31–33)? Have you publicly declared your faith in Christ through baptism?

_____

_____

_____

_____

What did Lydia do after her baptism that demonstrated her leadership, service, and hospitality?

_____

_____

_____

Everywhere the Apostle Paul went, he organized new believers into churches. Lydia's home soon became the gathering place for Christians in Philippi. Given the fact she had a house large enough to host Paul, Silas, Timothy, Luke, and servants (See "household" in Acts 16:15.), it became the natural place for the church to meet.

📖 What role did Lydia and her home play in Acts 16:40?

_____

_____

_____

📖 Read Romans 12:6–8 about spiritual gifts. What spiritual gift(s) did Lydia seem to have been given by God? What spiritual gift(s) has God given you?

_____

_____

_____

_____

_____

It is God's plan for His people to find one another and meet together, even if it is only "two or three" of you (Matthew 18:20). Indeed, Hebrews 10:24–25 exhorts us to meet together regularly to "consider how we may spur one another on toward love and good deeds." Every Christian should be part of a local assembly of believers—a church—for worship and fellowship, as well as joining together in a small group setting in which the personal work of accountability and discipleship can flourish.

God may want to use you, just as he used Lydia, to be the person who initiates a new Bible study, small group, ministry, or even a new church when one is needed. Faith in Christ is to be followed by "good works" (Ephesians 2:8–10). Lydia is a perfect example of that pattern being manifested for the good of those who lived in Philippi. God wants your life to be a personification of the faith-works pattern as well.

Responding to Scripture

📖 How would you describe the central idea of Acts 16:11–15?

_____

_____

Doctrine
BAPTISM

Jesus was baptized as a means of publicly identifying with John the Baptist's message of repentance and faith (Matthew 3:13–17). Jesus made baptism a sign of Christian conversion (Matthew 28:19–20).

"Don't ever come to church without coming as though it were the first time, as though it could be the best time and as though it might be the last time."

Vance Havner

_____

_____

_____

Responding to Life

What did you find in this passage that you could apply to your life immediately or in the days ahead?

_____

_____

_____

_____

Responding to God

 Heavenly Father, I thank You for men like Paul and his fellow-workers who endured hardships to spread the Gospel of Christ, so that ultimately I might receive Him and believe. Please help me to live like Lydia—to use the gifts You have given me to strengthen the body of Christ where I live. Help me find a place of ministry and service as an act of gratitude to You for opening my heart to believe in Jesus. In His name I pray. Amen.

Acts 16:6-40

DAY FOUR

GAINING TRUE FREEDOM (ACTS 16:16–40)

A dear friend of mine calls herself a "doubter." She says, "Nancy, I can rationalize away Christ in the midst of an intellectual debate. But when the plane is going down I will be the first one crying out, 'Lord, I believe, I believe!'" It's no wonder God shakes things up a bit in our lives. He wants to save us from ourselves—our apathy, our pride, our ignorance, our unbelief, and our spiritual passivity.

That's what happened to the man in charge of the jail in Philippi. Paul and Silas had been beaten and incarcerated for preaching about Jesus, when God sent an earthquake to shake up the jailer's worldview. When he cried out, "What must I do to be saved?" in the midst of the earthquake, his question probably had more than one meaning! He may have seen the earthquake as a sign of God's displeasure for the officials having treated His ambassadors so cruelly.

It's often said, "There are no atheists in foxholes," and "We don't realize God is all we need until He is all we have." It would be great if we could all find God without distress, but times of trouble can be an excellent catalyst to help us recognize how serious our need for God really is. The jailer received the answer to his question from the apostles he was guarding. The answer he received will work for anyone who wants to know, "What must I do to be saved?"

FREEDOM TAKEN TEMPORARILY

📖 *Acts 16:16–24 (Read this lengthy passage in your Bible.)*

It was not unusual for the Apostle Paul and other first-century Christians to suffer for their faith. In fact, in 2 Corinthians 6:4–10, 11:23–28, Paul defended himself as a true apostle of Christ by listing the ways he had suffered. Why would anyone suffer like that for something he knew was a lie?

In Philippi, Paul and Silas were beaten and thrown into jail for casting a demonic spirit out of a fortune-teller. Based on the charges levied against Paul and Silas in Acts 16:20–21, can you see parallels in today's culture? How are Christians around the world persecuted today for practices of which society doesn't approve?

_____

_____

_____

_____

All around the world today, Christians who live under oppressive governments are put in jail to silence their testimony. But that never works. As the early church father, Tertullian, wrote, "The blood of the martyrs is the seed of the church." Whenever the true church of Jesus Christ is persecuted, the church grows. That happened following the resurrection of Christ when the first church in Jerusalem was persecuted. "On that day a great persecution broke out against the church in Jerusalem, and all except the apostles were scattered throughout Judea and Samaria" (Acts 8:1). Seeds of faith are sown whenever the church is persecuted or scattered such as in the years the Communist government in China tried to extinguish the church by imprisoning Christians. But when the government began allowing religious expression, it was found that the church had multiplied many times over. Believers in jail or in underground networks had continued to witness for Christ in spite of their persecution.

Even though Paul and Silas were in an interior cell of the jail with their feet locked in stocks (Acts 16:24), they still had their spiritual freedom. How does Acts 16:25 demonstrate this?

_____

_____

_____

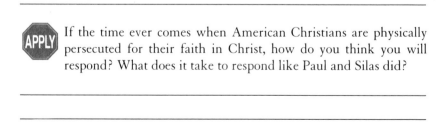 If the time ever comes when American Christians are physically persecuted for their faith in Christ, how do you think you will respond? What does it take to respond like Paul and Silas did?

_____

_____

_____

_____

 *Did You Know?*

DEMONIC ACTIVITY

The New Testament pictures Satan and his demonic angels as having access to planet earth, seeking access to human minds and hearts (1 John 5:19). But Christ came to "destroy the devil's work" (1 John 3:8). Evidence of this can be found in Jesus' many victories over demons as recorded in the four gospel accounts.

According to Voice of the Martyrs ministry, more than thirty nations today are classified as "Restricted," where access to the Gospel is limited and Christians are subject to oppression or persecution for their faith.

ROMAN CITIZENSHIP

In the Roman Empire, it was illegal for Roman citizens to be punished without due process of law. In Paul's and Silas's case, they were beaten and jailed on "hearsay," without inquiry being made about citizenship. Local magistrates could be punished by Rome for violating the rights of a Roman citizen, which both Paul and Silas were (Acts 22:28). When the Philippian magistrates learned they had punished two Roman citizens without trial, they released Paul and Silas quietly. But Paul insisted on a public release in order that their innocence would be evident to all.

Doctrine

SALVATION

There are two dimensions of salvation in the New Testament: instantaneous and ongoing. Acts 16:31 and Romans 10:9 illustrate the immediate aspect of salvation, while 1 Corinthians 1:18 and 2 Corinthians 2:15 illustrate the ongoing aspect. We are both "saved" and "being saved" by faith in Christ.

FREEDOM BESTOWED PERMANENTLY

📖 *Acts 16:25–40 (Read this lengthy passage in your Bible.)*

Even though Paul and Silas' physical freedom was taken away temporarily, they still had the ability to point others to spiritual freedom even while locked away in jail. Why were Paul and Silas a perfect illustration of the admonition of 2 Timothy 4:2?

_____

_____

_____

APPLY When the jailer cried out, "What must I do to be saved?" (Acts 16:30) what do you think he wanted to be saved from? What did you want to be saved from when you accepted Christ? How are things different in your life now?

Jailer: _____

You:_____

_____

_____

What was Paul's answer to the jailer (Acts 16:31)? In what ways was he saved?

_____

_____

_____

How do we know Paul's answer is for anyone who is "thirsty" and not just for the Philippian jailer (John 7:37–39)?

_____

_____

_____

_____

God always surprises us by those he saves, sometimes the most unlikely of characters. The Apostle Paul was the Jews' chief "hit man" against other Jews who became followers of Christ, traveling far and near to round up Jewish Christians and throw them in jail. Yet Jesus chose Paul to be His chief apostle—His chief trophy of grace.

John Newton, the author of the song, "Amazing Grace," was a profligate seafarer who profited from the trade in African slaves. Yet God chose him to become a pastor in England and author of the world's most beloved spiritual hymn.

Chuck Colson was Special Counsel to President Nixon and known as his "hatchet man". In 1971 he was found guilty of obstruction of justice during the Watergate Scandal. He became a Christian in 1973 and served seven months in the federal Maxwell Prison in Alabama. Colson's mid life conversion sparked a radical change in his life that led to the founding of Prison Fellowship ministry, dedicated to spreading the gospel into prisons across the country. As an evangelical Christian leader, Chuck was a sought after speaker and author of over 30 Christian books. Only the power of God can take a least-likely candidate from cunning liar to proclaimer of Truth.

The Philippian jailer might have seemed like an unlikely candidate for conversion to Christ, but the grace of God knows no boundaries. For what reasons would you have found yourself an unlikely target for God's grace?

_____

_____

_____

Responding to Scripture

What idea from this passage do you find to be most important?

_____

_____

_____

_____

Responding to Life

How can you apply that idea to your own life?

_____

_____

_____

_____

Responding to God

 Heavenly Father, thank You that no one can take away the freedom I have in Jesus Christ. Thank You that the joy available to me through You cannot be quenched by any difficult circumstance in life. And most of all, I thank You for extending Your grace and mercy to me. I know I could never deserve or earn my salvation. Thank You for making it a gift to me through faith in Jesus Christ. In His name I pray. Amen.

REVIEW FOR FOLLOWING GOD

One of the most interesting descriptions of the work of God found in the New Testament comes from Jesus himself, when He compared the work of the Holy Spirit to the wind: "The wind blows wherever it pleases. You hear its sound, but you cannot tell where it comes from or where it is going. So it is with everyone born of the Spirit" (John 3:8).

> "Assurance does not lie in what we are, be we great or small. It lies in what God has done in his plan of salvation to secure us to himself."
>
> **Sinclair Ferguson**

> "The recognition of sin is the beginning of salvation."
>
> **Martin Luther**

Acts 16:6-40

DAY FIVE

Put Yourself in Their Shoes

PAUL'S SECOND MISSIONARY JOURNEY

The cities or regions Paul and his companions visited on this, his second missionary journey, included these, to which he ultimately wrote letters: Galatia, Philippi, Thessalonica, Corinth, and Ephesus.

"As the soldier follows his general, as the servant follows his master, as the scholar follows his teacher, as the sheep follows its shepherd, just so ought the professing Christian to follow Christ."

J. C. Ryle

When the wind has blown hard, we can see where it has been. And we can feel and see its present effects. But as for the future, we cannot predict its strength or movement with any kind of accuracy; it "blows where it pleases." We see this principle worked out in the lives of Paul and his ministry companions. They set out from Syrian Antioch to visit churches in Asia Minor and had their path blocked twice by God in that region, only to have a clear door open to enter Macedonia (present-day Europe). As far as we know from Scripture, this was not their plan; they did not see the wind of the Spirit blowing that way.

But they did not argue with the change in plans; they simply allowed the Spirit to carry them along. Because they were obedient, they found themselves accomplishing greater ministry objectives than they had planned on–in Philippi, Thessalonica, Corinth, Ephesus, and many smaller cities in between, before returning to Jerusalem and Antioch.

In this book, we are studying the relationship Paul developed with the church in one of those cities: Philippi. We're learning how the church was founded and what we can learn from the letter Paul wrote later to them. In this first week, we have focused on living the kind of life Paul lived when it came to following God's call—a flexible life, which stays sensitive to the movement of God. We are learning to yield to closed doors and to walk through the open ones, to walk by faith rather than by sight, to be willing to be used by God, regardless of the circumstances.

REVIEW OF DAY 1: GUIDED TOWARD PHILIPPI (ACTS 16:6)

When I committed my life to Christ in 1985 in response to a challenge by a Bible teacher, little did I know how the plan for my life would change. My pre-Christian life plan was predictable for a young women like myself: live a morally upright life, be a loving wife, raise successful children, and be a conscientious member of my community and church. That was the plan when Nancy was in charge. When I asked Christ to be Lord of my life, things changed. None of the previous goals were eliminated, but they all had a new motivation. One big goal was added that I never saw coming.

My hunger to know the Bible seemed insatiable. I took as many Bible classes as I could at our church and devoured books and resources by trusted Bible teachers. A few years later, church leaders asked me to start a small class for women to help them study the Bible. I agreed and began with a group of fourteen women. By the next year, a waiting list had formed, so the church allowed me to open the doors to even more women. To make a twenty-year story short, today more than five hundred women are involved in that ongoing weekly Bible study.

Looking back, I didn't know enough to say no. In my rookie enthusiasm, I just kept walking through open doors, figuring it was what Christians were supposed to do. Of course, there have been challenges and bumps along the way and even a few closed doors. But I've gradually learned that God is like the wind. It's better to stop predicting where He goes and just learn to go with the flow–*His* flow.

APPLY What has been the biggest surprise God has orchestrated in your life since becoming a Christian? How well have you managed in following his lead?

_____

_____

_____

_____

REVIEW OF DAY 2: GETTING TO MACEDONIA (ACTS 16:7–10)

In my own life, and my conversations with other women through the years, one of the biggest questions I encounter is, "How do I know God's will?" We all want to obey God faithfully, but sometimes we wish God was clearer about issues not expressly covered in Scripture. To put it simply, I've concluded that God leads us in a way that is similar to how parents lead their children. Sometimes we tell our children exactly what we want them to do, and sometimes we let them weigh the options and make their own decisions, even if their choices require a little course correction along the way. We, and our children, grow and mature as those two approaches are worked out over time.

Someone once said, "If it's Monday, and you want to know what God's will for Tuesday is, wait until Wednesday." In other words, God has a way of working out His will in our lives through His leading, our choices, and our mistakes, even if we don't recognize His will until after the fact.

📖 What assurances for walking in God's will do you find in Proverbs 3:5–6? What result does Philippians 4:6–7 promise if you trust him?

_____

_____

_____

_____

REVIEW OF DAY 3: GATEWAY TO CONVERSION (ACTS 16:11–15)

Because you and I are not apostles, we don't often see ourselves as being responsible for witnessing to others about Christ. Yet we encounter people in our world daily who don't know Christ. If God has put us in their path, who's to say we are not the one who should share Christ with them?

When he arrived in a new town like Philippi, Paul always went to the same place: the Jewish synagogue. The Jews were his people. He could speak their social and religious language; they were his nearest affinity group. Since there was no synagogue in Philippi, he went to where God-fearing people met on the Sabbath. He and his friends joined their group and engaged them in conversation about Jesus and won Lydia and her household to the Lord. Sure, Lydia could have said, "No thanks," as many had responded to Paul. But Paul didn't worry. His job was to go where Jesus wasn't known and announce the Good News in a way people could understand linguistically, socially, and religiously.

Who is your closest affinity group? Don't forget your own "household" and extended family. What progress have you made in sharing Jesus with them?

_____

_____

_____

Word Study
OIKOS

The Greek word for house or household is *oikos*. Oikos evangelism is a phrase used to refer to the way the gospel travels most easily—to those in one's "house" or affinity group, with whom connections are natural and respected, providing credibility and a hearing for "gossiping" the Gospel.

> "By God's grace, I make myself available today to follow God's leading in my life; to serve Him by serving others for the progress of the Gospel and His glory."

Initials: _____

Date: _____

REVIEW OF DAY 4: GAINING TRUE FREEDOM (ACTS 16:16–40)

A recurring theme in Scripture is that it costs us something to give something to another. The biblical word for that theme is "sacrifice". In Philippi, Paul and Silas gave up their health and comfort (they were beaten by city officials) and their freedom (they were put in jail) in order that the Philippian jailer and his family might find spiritual and eternal freedom in Christ. Paul and Silas didn't know the situation would work out that way, but they had an ongoing, predetermined commitment to pay whatever price was asked of them in order to be faithful to the calling of Christ that others might gain the freedom they were willing to give up.

Have you counted the cost of what it means to be a follower of Jesus (Luke 14:28–33)? Is there any price Jesus might ask you to pay that you are not yet ready to pay? Compose your own brief prayer to God, expressing your true feelings on the cost of following Christ. Ask God for whatever you need in this area.

_____
_____
_____
_____
_____
_____
_____
_____

REVIEW ACTS 16:6–40

Review the scriptures and content of this week's lessons and identify three ideas, themes, or action points that strike you from what you studied this week. Especially look for ideas to apply to your own life.

1. _____
_____
_____
_____
_____

2. _____
_____
_____
_____
_____

3. _____
_____
_____

_____

_____

REFLECT ON ACTS 16:31

They replied, "Believe in the Lord Jesus, and you will be saved—you and your household."

What can you do in your home to claim this verse for yourself and your family?

_____

_____

_____

_____

REMEMBER GOD'S GRACE IN YOUR LIFE

 Heavenly Father, thank You for working through the Apostle Paul and others to spread the Gospel of Jesus throughout the world. Thank You for bringing the Gospel message to me. Help me to see the open doors You place before me. Let me walk through them and share Christ's Good News with others. In Jesus' name I pray. Amen.

Notes

Notes

Philippians 1 : 1 – 11

LESSON OVERVIEW
ENTRANCE INTO FELLOWSHIP

A man named John slowly disappeared from the church he attended. He stopped attending Bible study. He gave up getting together with church friends and skipped a men's event he'd been invited to. His absence was so gradual that few people noticed he was no longer around.

But the pastor of John's church noticed, and he stopped by John's house one evening. John invited the pastor in to join him in front of the fire. The pastor listened patiently as John told him how he preferred to worship God surrounded by nature rather than surrounded by a lot of judgmental people. As John talked, the pastor reached out with a fireplace shovel and pulled a hot coal out of the fire onto the hearth. As John spoke about being an introvert and preferring to be alone, the coal cooled, its light dwindling, until eventually it was barely warm. Then the pastor pushed the coal back into the fire and it began to glow again as it absorbed heat from the embers around it. The pastor's unspoken message made its way to John's heart.

The pastor never had to say a word. Seeing that his point had been made, he politely ended the conversation and stood to leave. As the pastor left, John said, "I'll see you Sunday, Pastor." God created us to live in community. Paul makes this clear in the book of Philippians. The one who began a good work in us intended for that work to continue in the context of community. One of the ways we learn how to live with God is by living with the people in whom He dwells.

GRACE AND PEACE (PHILIPPIANS 1:1-2)

In 1765 John Fawcett was called to pastor a small congregation at Wainsgate, England. He labored there diligently for seven years on a meager salary. When he received a call to a much larger congregation, he decided to accept it. As the few possessions that he and his wife owned were loaded on their wagon, the church members came by and begged them to stay.

Touched by the outpouring of love, he and his wife began to weep. Mrs. Fawcett exclaimed, "Oh, John, I just cannot bear this. They need us so badly here." And Fawcett said, "God has spoken to my heart as well. Tell them to unload the wagon." This experience inspired Fawcett to write the classic hymn, "Blest Be the Tie," the first line of which says, "Blest be the tie that binds our hearts in Christian love; the fellowship of kindred minds is like to that above."[2]

One of the greatest joys of a Christian's life is entering into fellowship with other Christians. The word "fellowship" means "to have in common." As a fellow believer and follower of Christ, you walk alongside others who share a common trust in Christ as their Savior as well as people with a common set of principles.

The Apostle Paul enjoyed that kind of relationship with the church in Philippi. On more than one occasion, the Philippian church sent gifts to Paul in support of his ministry, especially when he was incarcerated in Rome (Philippians 4:10–19). Paul's thank-you letter to the Philippians expanded into a heartfelt primer on contentment and joy in the Christian life, not only for the first century but for the twenty-first century as well.

SERVANTS AND SAINTS

> *Paul and Timothy, servants of Christ Jesus, to all the saints in Christ Jesus at Philippi, together with the overseers and deacons: (Philippians 1:1)*

Has anyone ever responded to a favor you did by saying, "Thank you! You are such a saint to do that for me?" You may have felt a twinge of guilt because you certainly didn't feel like a saint. Maybe just that morning you had spent extra time confessing your sins to God. Aren't saints people like Mother Teresa?

It's not biblical to judge a person as a saint on the basis of actions. In Philippians 1:1, Paul calls every Christian in Philippi a saint. It's likely he didn't even know many of them or the quality of their spiritual lives. So why were they "saints"?

In the New Testament, the word "saint" means "holy one" and refers to a person's position before God—not his actions. In the Old Testament, the word "holy" was applied to many common, everyday objects—even pagan temple prostitutes—because they had been set aside for a specific purpose. Dr. J. Vernon McGee said, "Even the old pots and pans in the tabernacle were called 'holy vessels' though they were probably beaten and worn-out after 40 years in the desert. However, they had been 'set apart' for God's use."[3]

Doctrine
SAINTS

When Paul calls the Philippian believers "saints," he is not referring to them as in the Roman Catholic tradition–venerated Christians from church history recognized for their works. Instead, in the New Testament, all Christians are saints. The word "saint" simply means "holy one." Even though we are not always holy in practice, God views us as called out and set apart for Himself—a holy one in position and hopefully in practice.

Doctrine
ELDERS AND DEACONS (PHILIPPIANS 1:1)

There were two categories of leaders in the early church: elders (overseers) and deacons. Elders were referred to as overseers (as here) or shepherds (1 Peter 5:2) and are always referred to in the plural in the context of a local church (Acts 14:23). The apostle Paul set forth qualifications for elders and deacons in 1 Timothy 3:1–13. Deacons were apparently an outgrowth of the seven men chosen to handle supporting tasks in the first church in Jerusalem (Acts 6:1–4).

In light of this truth, why could Paul refer to all the Christians at Philippi as saints?

_____

_____

_____

It is not the way we live our life that qualifies us as saints, but rather the way Christ lived His life. Because Christ never sinned (Matthew 4:10–11; Hebrews 4:15; Hebrews 7:26–28), He was holy in practice and position. Even demons recognized him as "the Holy One of God!" (Mark 1:24). Paul refers to the Christians at Philippi as being "in Christ," and that's what makes them saints, or holy ones (Colossians 3:3). It is our faith in God's true Holy One, Jesus Christ, that cleanses us from our sin in God's sight and allows us to be called holy as well.

"In Christ" means two things in the New Testament: where we place our faith and where God sees us. We believe "in Christ" in order to become God's child and a follower of Jesus (Galatians 3:26). From the moment we first believe, God sees us as "in Christ" with respect to our sins (Romans 8:1). We share in Christ's holiness. Even when we sin, God sees us as forgiven and holy in His sight because He sees us "in Christ."

 How do you know that you are "in Christ" today?

_____

_____

_____

GRACE AND PEACE

Grace and peace to you from God our Father and the Lord Jesus Christ. (Philippians 1:2)

Standard greetings today can run from formal ("How are you?"), to informal ("How's it going?"), to familiar ("What's up?"), to very familiar ("'Sup?"). Our greetings are mainly conversation starters or polite gestures. In biblical days, greetings were more meaningful. The words were deeper, and they were spoken almost like a blessing. "Grace and peace to you" was the most common greeting among New Testament writers: Paul used it ten times; Peter used it twice, and John used it once. "Grace, mercy, and peace" was used twice by Paul and once by John.

In addition to its use in letters, "grace" (*charis* in Greek) also was a common spoken greeting, as if the person were to say, "Have a blessed day" or "Blessings be upon you." Grace was the most distinctive theological idea in the New Testament. The English word "grace" appears only eight times in the Old Testament, but it appears 123 times in the New Testament.

"Peace" is the New Testament version of the Hebrew idea of *shalom*—peace, wholeness, or soundness. "Shalom" is used by Jews today as a greeting—a wish for peace and wholeness for those they meet. The root of the word "shalom" is seen in the name Jeru*salem*, or "city of peace." Ironically, Jerusalem is the most embattled city in the world and will not know true peace until the Prince of Peace returns.

Doctrine
IN CHRIST

The phrase "in Christ" occurs 91 times in the English (NIV) New Testament. Paul's promise of peace is to those who are "in Christ Jesus" (Philippians 4:7). Being "in Christ" simply means believing in Christ, being counted as a true believer, being baptized into Christ Jesus by the Holy Spirit (1 Corinthians 12:13). So the prerequisite for the peace of God is faith in Christ.

Grace is receiving goodness that we do not deserve.

Mercy is not receiving punishment we do deserve.

Peace is living in the reality of mercy and grace.

The "peace" Paul used as a written greeting was not a reference to circumstantial peace, but a reminder of the peace of God extended to every Christian. It was a way of saying, "I trust you are walking in the peace of God, which life in Christ makes possible" (Philippians 4:6–7).

📖 What was your status with God before becoming a Christian? (Romans 5:10a; Colossians 1:21)

_____

_____

_____

_____

📖 What is necessary before one can have and experience peace with God (Romans 5:1)?

_____

_____

_____

📖 In light of Ephesians 2:8–9, do you think there is a reason Paul said "grace and peace" instead of "peace and grace?"

_____

_____

_____

Put Yourself in Their Shoes
THANKFUL APOSTLE

Paul expressed thanks in prayer and in person for many of the Christians to whom he wrote: the Romans (1:8), those at Corinth (1 Corinthians 1:4), the Colossians (1:3), the Thessalonicans (1 Thessalonians 1:2; 2 Thessalonians 1:3), Timothy (2 Timothy 1:3), and Philemon (verse 4).

Responding to Scripture

📖 What is Paul's overall purpose in Philippians 1:1–2?

_____

_____

_____

_____

What did Paul want the Philippians to know or understand about this purpose?

_____

_____

_____

Responding to Life

What is the main idea or truth you can take away from this lesson—a truth that will impact your life today?

_____

_____

_____

_____

Heavenly Father, thank You that, by your grace, I can have peace with You today through the Lord Jesus Christ. Thank You for viewing me as a saint—a holy one—in spite of my sins and imperfections. I pray today to walk in Your grace and peace and to live my life as one set apart for Your service. In Christ's name I pray, Amen.

GRATITUDE AND AFFECTION (PHILIPPIANS 1:3–5)

Philippians 1:1-11

DAY TWO

My daughter, Meggie, and her husband, David, belong to a wonderful faith community. I knew early on this was the case. While they were on their honeymoon, friends from their church came to their new little house (which was desperate for renovation) and applied a fresh coat of paint to the interior walls. You can imagine their gratitude and the love they felt when they returned home to a freshly painted house.

What if you were the only Christian in your community? Life would be a bit more challenging, wouldn't it? The fellowship of other believers is one of those aspects of life we sometimes take for granted, but one we would sorely miss if it was suddenly removed.

The Apostle Paul had good reason to be thankful for the Christian believers in Philippi. They had reached out to him while he was under house arrest in Rome, supplying him with material support, fellowship, and encouragement. He was so touched by their presence in his life that it is the first thing he mentions as he begins his letter to them.

GRATITUDE EXPRESSED IN PRAYER

> *I thank my God every time I remember you. In all my prayers for all of you, I always pray with joy. (Philippians 1:3–4)*

One day, a large basket arrived at my front door. It was filled with hundreds of handwritten notes from the women of my Bible study who had written to me for Valentine's Day. I can't tell you what their kindness meant to me. I slowly read each one, and I remember how many of them quoted Philippians 1:3: "I thank my God every time I remember you."

There is nothing like a dear friend in Christ. I believe you can know someone your entire life and yet not experience anything close to the bonds of a Christian friend you might have known only six months. There is transparency, acceptance, and understanding in Christian relationships, because every true believer has experienced the same humbling (guilty of sin) and lifting up (redeemed by grace). Everyone is on equal footing and common ground before God. My friends within the faith community mean the world to me. Their prayers, support, and encouragement are priceless riches, impossible to find among those whose first loyalty is to something or someone other than God.

Likewise, the Philippians came to Paul's mind often, and every time they did he thanked God for them. Paul's attitude of gratitude toward his brothers and sisters in Christ is what every Christian should imitate.

APPLY When was the last time you expressed gratitude in a specific way to or for another Christian, either in person or in prayer?

_____

_____

_____

Why should we be grateful for other believers in general, even when they have done nothing specific for us?

_____

_____

_____

Most people sitting in prison would be writing others to ask for prayers for themselves. But Paul remained focused on praying for others, even in his own time of need. Paul was demonstrating the principle he wrote in 1 Corinthians 10:24: "Nobody should seek his own good, but the good of others." Explain what Paul meant in that verse. Should we never seek our own good in life?

_____

_____

_____

_____

What principles found in John 13:34–35 and John 15:13 did Paul exemplify?

_____

_____

_____

Even when we are not in physical proximity to those who are in need, why is prayer our single best means of serving them?

_____

_____

_____

A particular friend in Christ demonstrates this kind of concern for others. Cindy is known for her hugs, her love notes, and her joy in making others laugh. Even when faced with a crisis in her own life—her husband's terminal cancer—she never stopped loving others, never stopped showing gratitude, and was always available to the many friends who depended on her as a source of strength. She continued to pray for others even when she was the one who likely needed prayers the most. That is the love of Christ. It was also the love of Christ in Paul that led him to pray for others, even while in difficult circumstances.

In the New International Version translation of the Bible (1994 version), the word "joy" and various forms of "rejoice" occur fourteen times in the four short chapters of Philippians. How did Paul manifest the intended result of all Jesus taught His disciples (John 15:11)?

_____

_____

_____

📖 In Psalm 16:11, where did the psalmist say he found joy?

_____

_____

Did You Know?
JOY

"Joy" is a concept we find throughout Philippians. It's in all of these verses: 1:4, 25–26; 2:2, 29; 4:1.

And the word "rejoice" can be found in verses 1:18; 2:17–18; 3:1; 4:4, 10.

These two words occur a total of 44 times in all of Paul's epistles. Philippians is often referred to as "The Epistle of Joy."

As a new Christian, one of the first books I read was *The Christian's Secret to a Happy Life* by Hannah Whitall Smith. The "secret" about which she wrote was being "hid in Christ," being totally surrendered to God and His purposes. A person hidden in Christ experiences true joy—joy that is rooted in Jesus Christ and His love for us—especially while we experience great difficulties. Jesus said, "I have told you these things, so that in me you may have peace. In this world you will have trouble. But take heart! I have overcome the world" (John 16:33). This theme is what fuels Paul's entire message throughout Philippians.

Thankful for Persevering Partners in the Gospel

Because of your partnership in the gospel from the first day until now. (Philippians 1:5)

Would you have considered your partners in the Gospel a source of joy as Paul did? List your top three reasons for giving thanks for your partners in the Christian life. Why are you thankful for them?

1. _____

_____

_____

_____

2. _____

_____

_____

_____

3. _____

_____

_____

_____

At times when I am surrounded by those who are apathetic about their faith, I think about how I would fare if I were the only Christian in the world. How strong would I be? Could I be faithful without the encouragement of others, my co-laborers and partners in the Christian life? I seriously doubt it. When considering that possibility, I'm immediately made aware of how thankful I am for the fellow followers of Jesus who are part of my life. Here's how I would answer that last question above:

1. My family. I'm sure I sometimes take for granted the privilege and blessing of having a husband and four grown children who are Christ-followers. While each one of us grow in our own way as we try to follow Jesus, we can still pray for one another, be accountable to each other, and support one another in our faith. I am thankful for the shared faith of my family.

2. The leaders of the Women's Community Bible Study of Atlanta. I am often humbled by the commitment, maturity, and thoughtfulness of the women who form the leadership core of our Bible study. They are wise and willing and serve as continual sources of inspiration for me. From the church to the family and ministries in between, God has established a plurality of leaders as His design. I am thankful for the strength I get from the women with whom I serve.

3. The larger body of Christ. Every Christian is a "cell" in the Body of Christ that gains health and strength from every other strong cell. Whenever I am in a large gathering of Christians, whether it's my church, a conference, or a mission trip, I look around and realize I am part of something good and great that God is doing in the world. I realize there are many faithful believers—some I know, most I don't—who are persevering in the faith for Jesus' sake. I am so thankful for each one and for how I am encouraged by their faith.

Responding to Scripture

What is Paul's main idea in Philippians 1:3–6?

_____

_____

_____

_____

Summarize Paul's explanation of that idea in your own words:

_____

_____

_____

_____

Responding to Life

How should the truth of these verses impact your response to challenges and difficulties you face in life? How might you use these verses to comfort another Christian who is going through a difficult time?

_____

_____

_____

_____

Heavenly Father, I thank You for my fellow Christians who care for me and to whom I can minister with the love of Christ. Please help me remember to show them my gratitude in word and deed. I praise and thank You that you began the work of faith in me, and You will bring it to completion; I don't have to depend on my efforts to save myself. Grant me the grace to rest in Your all-sufficient arms—to see every aspect of life as something You are using to conform me to Christ. In His name I pray, Amen.

GOOD WORKS WITHIN (PHILIPPIANS 1:6–8)

Philippians 1:1–11

DAY THREE

The epitaph on the tombstone of the late Ruth Bell Graham reads "End of construction. Thank you for your patience." These were words she chose herself from a construction sign. Mrs. Graham believed this was "a marvelous image for the Christian life, a work under construction until we go to be with God."

Being conformed to the image of Jesus Christ (Romans 8:29) is a lifelong process. None of us has arrived; all of us are under construction. It's important to remember this fact about ourselves, but perhaps even more important to remember the same for those we come in contact with. Sometimes we are quick to forgive ourselves but not so quick to forgive others. Others of us struggle to get past our failings.

All of this is why Philippians 1:6 is so comforting. We consistently fail to live up to God's standards of righteousness, and we wonder if we are making any spiritual progress at all. We wonder if God will stick with us while we stumble through this life. We get tired of confessing our sins and witnessing the sins of those close to us. We wonder if God gets tired of hearing us. We are worn out and weighed down by sin, sometimes so much that we're almost embarrassed to ask God's forgiveness…again!

But verses like Philippians 1:6 and 1 Thessalonians 5:24 correct our unbiblical thinking. Who is committed to ensuring our spiritual progress–and arriving at our ultimate spiritual destination? God is.

COMPLETE AND CONFIDENT

Being confident of this, that he who began a good work in you will carry it on to completion until the day of Christ Jesus. (Philippians 1:6)

How does Jesus' metaphor of the vine and branches in John 15:1–8 illustrate that our spiritual life draws on a divine source other than ourselves?

_____

_____

_____

"Have you ever noticed the difference in the Christian life between work and fruit? A machine can do work; only a life can bear fruit."

Andrew Murray

Put Yourself in Their Shoes
FELLOWSHIP

To be arrested and imprisoned, as Paul was when he wrote to the Philippians, would have been a matter of great shame in his day; the equivalent of being a criminal. But the Philippians stood with Paul; they did not abandon him in his hour of trouble. Since fellowship refers to having all things in common (including suffering), it was as if the Philippians were in jail themselves. When Paul suffered, they suffered. This was the source of Paul's affection for them.

_____
_____
_____
_____
_____
_____

You and I can rest in these promises. It is not up to us to grow. It is up to us to be obedient and depend on Christ in all aspects of our lives. Any good work that comes from us is His doing. Branches can produce no fruit on their own, regardless of their effort, concentration, or sincere desire. Only by their union with the vine, from which comes life, can the branches bear fruit.

📖 According to Jesus, how much can we accomplish on our own, apart from Him (John 15:5b)?

_____

📖 What is our responsibility in the process of growth (John 15:7)?

_____
_____

📖 How do the two verses in Romans 8:28–29 support God's role in our spiritual growth as summarized in Philippians 1:6?

Romans 8:29, the goal:

_____
_____

Romans 8:28, God's part:

_____
_____

Here is the good news: We can be confident that no matter how sinful we feel, or how often we fail, Jesus is full of mercy. He will forgive us and will continue to work everything "for the good of those who love him." God's work _for_ us began when Christ died on the cross and was raised from the dead. His work _in_ us begins when we accept Christ as our Savior and the Holy Spirit comes to dwell in us. And his work _through_ us begins as we depend on the Spirit in our daily walk.
What measure of confidence do these verses on growth give you, especially in moments when you feel like a failure?

_____
_____
_____
_____

Fill in the blank: I am confident of this, that he who began a good work in (your name)_____ will carry it on to completion until the day of Christ Jesus. Now take this sentence, memorize it, and hang it somewhere so you will be reminded of God's faithfulness.

It is right for me to feel this way about all of you, since I have you in my heart; for whether I am in chains or defending and confirming the gospel, all of you share in God's grace with me. God can testify how I long for all of you with the affection of Christ Jesus. (Philippians 1:7–8)

Christian friendship is a treasure unlike any other friendship. When Christ is at the center, the bond goes deep. There is a natural sense of acceptance, forgiveness, and encouragement. We recognize that everyone sins, even our closest friends, and that we all need Jesus' forgiveness, not to mention each other's. On one hand, we walk in humility together, and on the other hand, we walk in total joy, because we have all experienced grace and mercy. A beautiful combination of humility and joy usually governs every friendship founded on Christ.

To experience true Christian friendship is to experience the unconditional love of God. When we experience the forgiveness of Christ in our own lives, it naturally overflows to others. Paul and the Philippians experienced the grace and mercy of Christ and freely gave it to one another.

I know women who have succumbed to the busyness of the world and had no time to gather with their Christian friends. A year or so later they came to realize nothing could replace being surrounded and uplifted by Christ-centered friends. Even if you don't have time for all the activities you once attended at church, the importance of time with those who can build you up in the faith is irreplaceable. Nothing comes close to the natural grace that Christian friends extend to one another. Friends in Christ don't love you because of what you do or who you have become. They love you in spite of what you do and have become–the same way God in Christ loves us (Ephesians 4:32).

Paul and the Philippian Christians were partners in Christ (as we will see in detail in Philippians 4). They were Christian friends. Their bond was strong, and their love was deep. Paul naturally missed them and "longed for all of [them] with the affection of Christ Jesus.

There is a real feeling that develops when you serve alongside someone in Jesus' name. It's in some ways miraculous and indescribable, but how would you describe it if you had to?

_____

_____

_____

_____

📖 Summarize the teaching of Hebrews 10:24–25. Explain some things Christians should do with their words when they come together.

_____

_____

_____

_____

Doctrine
FRIENDSHIP

Friendship was a covenant term. In the Old Covenant, Abraham was the friend of God (Isaiah 41:8; James 2:23). In the New Covenant, the disciples became the friends of God (John 15:13–15). Proverbs 18:24 says there is a friend "who sticks closer than a brother," as Jonathan did when David was in trouble (1 Samuel 19—20). Friends united by faith in Christ share a bond deeper than any other.

Responding to Scripture

📖 In one sentence or short phrase, what is the central theme of Philippians 1:6–8?

_____

_____

_____

Responding to Life

What did you learn in this lesson that will make the biggest impact on your life?

_____

_____

_____

_____

_____

Responding to God

 Heavenly Father, how incomprehensible that You love me as much as You do! I stumble each day, yet You love me in spite of who I am. Thank You for my fellow believers in Christ through whom I can experience the love of Christ. I am so grateful for all You and those in my faith community mean to me. I also thank You that You are always at work in me to transform me into the image of Your Son Jesus and You will continue that work until the day He returns. Father, how incomprehensible is Your love for me in Jesus Christ! Amen.

Philippians 1:1–11

DAY FOUR

GIFT OF PRAYER (PHILIPPIANS 1:9–11)

Because my husband was involved in television news media for many years, we witnessed the evolution of the "sound bite," that short summary of a position captured in an interview and played on the evening news. Now Facebook and Twitter are teaching us how to summarize life in 140 characters or less.

Short summaries are good, and God uses them. The Ten Commandments, for example, are a summary of God's moral laws. Jesus further summarized the ten with two: love God and love your neighbor (Matthew 22:34–40). When we come to the Christian life, it's helpful to find summaries of what it's all about such as Paul's words in Philippians 1:9–11. Paul wanted the Philippian Christians to grow in their Christian life, so he prayed three things for them. Anyone who realizes Paul's three prayers for the Philippians in their own life will live as a spiritually mature Christian—one who loves, exercises spiritual discernment, and lives a pure and righteous life. A Christian who lives that way will live as Christ lived.

PRAYER FOR LOVE

And this is my prayer: that your love may abound more and more in knowl-edge and depth of insight. (Philippians 1:9)

Perhaps the deepest expression of love in a Christian friendship is when we pray to God for each other's needs (Hebrews 4:16). Paul wanted the Philippian believers to grow in their love. The *Today's English Version* (GNT) translation says, "I pray that your love will keep on growing more and more…"

But Paul wasn't talking about touchy-feely "luv," he was talking about bib-lical love. In what two characteristics of love did Paul want the Philippians to grow "more and more?"

_____ and _____

Growing in "knowledge and depth of insight" enables believers to love the way God loves–to love with a Christ-like love.

I have always wanted to be someone who is kind and loving to everyone I meet. I never realized how much the time I spent loving God would affect my ability to love others. But unfortunately, with age and experience comes caution and distrust of strangers. Sometimes a selfish desire to just "do my own thing" develops. I would justify my lack of attentiveness to the grocery store attendant, bank clerk, mailman, and others by telling myself I might be intruding in their busy day. But I gradually realized that was just a flimsy excuse. I was more concerned about my own agenda than whether they needed a friendly smile or a helping hand at that moment.

I learned something about how to love by watching my youngest daughter Mary, who seemed never to have met a stranger in her life! As the youngest of four children, she had been loved by so many for so long that she was nat-urally convinced that everyone loved her, which we did. Mary had no reser-vations in approaching those outside our family and was genuinely interest-ed in their lives. There was no fear of how they would respond to her. Her confidence in loving and reaching out to others, I learned, was based on the fact that she knew she was loved. She had been so filled with love that she had to share it.

The more confident we become in God's love for us by reading about it in His Word and by experiencing it through fellow believers, the more secure we will be in extending his love to others.

Paul prayed a similar prayer for the Ephesians. What were the four dimen-sions of God's love Paul wanted them to grasp (Ephesians 3:18)?

To know the _____ , _____, _____ , and _____ of God's love.

Next, Paul wanted the Philippians' love to be manifested in two ways: dis-cernment and purity.

PRAYER FOR DISCERNMENT

So that you may be able to discern what is best. (Philippians 1:10a)

Note Paul's words "so that." What was the first manifestation of knowledge and insight that Paul desired for the Philippians?

_____
_____
_____
_____

Word Study
DISCERNMENT

Several words in the New Testament can be translated by discern or discernment. *Diakrino* means to judge; *dokimazo* means to test or approve; and *aisthesei* means judgment or perception. All have the idea of separating what is right or righteous from what is not.

"God never gives us discernment in order that we may criticize, but that we may intercede."

Oswald Chambers

Discernment results from the heart and mind working together–something that takes time to learn. I know, at least, it took me a long time.

Years ago, when my children were young, I waited in my car in the carpool lane at their school. A woman in raggedy clothes and her toddler approached my car window and asked if I might give the two of them a ride to their apartment (on the other side of town). So, after collecting my children, we set out for her apartment. On the way, she told me she needed seventy-five dollars to avoid being evicted, so I dutifully provided the money, feeling sure I had shown her Christ's love.

A week later, again in the carpool lane, I noticed the same woman and toddler talking to another woman, who appeared to turn her away. A little suspicious, I spoke with the other woman and asked if she had given the lady money. She said she hadn't because she had seen the woman before and discovered that she was not telling the truth about her situation. The lesson I learned that day is that discernment is as much a part of love as is compassion. I learned that sometimes there are other loving ways to help in addition to giving someone money. Praying for Jesus to guide this woman through her plight also might have been a valuable way to give her what she most needed.

Discerning what is best is all about making the right moral and spiritual choices in life, living the kind of life described in Proverbs, learning the skill of living. That kind of wisdom and discernment doesn't come overnight, but it can be acquired. Again, the method is prayer.

Why not say a prayer right now and list the characteristics here that you hope God will build in you:

_____
_____
_____

📖 God wants us to come to him for assistance with discernment. What does James 1:5 say we should do to acquire wisdom?

_____
_____

How should spiritual discernment make choosing what is best a different process for the Christian than the non-Christian?

_____
_____
_____
_____

PRAYER FOR PURITY

And may be pure and blameless until the day of Christ, filled with the fruit of righteousness that comes through Jesus Christ—to the glory and praise of God. (Philippians 1:10b–11)

Discerning what is best is the first manifestation of knowledge and insight. What is the second and what would that look like?

_____

_____

_____

📖 Just like plants, every person produces fruit in his or her life. The question is what kind of fruit are we producing? Galatians 5:19–23 provides two lists of "fruit," traits or characteristics of a person's life. One list is the fruit ("acts") of unrighteousness that flow from the sinful human nature. List a few examples from this list in Galatians 19–21.

_____

_____

_____

_____

The second list is the fruit of the Holy Spirit—or righteous fruit. List all nine dimensions of this fruit (Galatians 22–23):

_____

_____

_____

_____

_____

Obviously, the second list is the list Paul is talking about to the Philippians–fruit or works produced by the life of God in a person who is committed to Christ and in whom lives the Holy Spirit. Paul prayed that the Philippians' knowledge and insight would lead to this kind of life–a pure and righteous life–"to the glory and praise of God."

This prayer was a high priority for Paul. We ought to make it a priority for ourselves and others as well that we might grow in love, in discernment, and in purity of heart and hands. When we are confident in God's love for us, our confidence in loving others and living righteously will increase.

Responding to Scripture

📖 Carefully summarize, in a phrase or sentence, Paul's main theme in Philippians 1:9–11?

_____

_____

_____

_____

Responding to Life

What could you do to apply Paul's message to your own life today or this week?

_____

_____

_____

_____

_____

Responding to God

 Father in heaven, I pray I might "grasp how wide and long and high and deep is the love of Christ, and to know this love that surpasses knowledge—that I may be filled to the measure of all the fullness of God." I pray that by knowing Your love, I may love others as You love them; that I may grow in knowledge and insight; that I may gain discernment; and that I might live a "pure and blameless" life until Christ returns. Because I know these things are Your will, I trust You will make them happen, every day, day by day. In Christ's name I pray. Amen.

Philippians 1:1-11

REVIEW FOR FOLLOWING GOD

Every Christian has been placed, by the Holy Spirit, in a community within the Body of Christ (1 Corinthians 12:13). We are called to exercise our spiritual gifts and manifest the fruit of the Spirit in that community, to love and encourage one another toward Christ-likeness. It's a community the world knows nothing of, like an elderly neighbor lady who used to pass our home on her daily walk through the neighborhood.

One day as she was passing by, a large group of women from our Bible study was leaving our house following a meeting. As everyone walked to their cars, she asked me what was going on. I told her it was a group of leaders from our Bible study, and she replied, as she turned to walk away, that she didn't believe in any kind of organized religion. I couldn't help but notice the contrast: a solitary, elderly woman walking away from a community of laughing, hugging women. Sadly, too many people see Christianity as an organized religion rather than a community of people who love Jesus and one another.

By design, people are happiest in community. God made the Body of Christ for that very reason. We can dry up spiritually if we don't seek the company of other believers. Just like little babies will fail to thrive if they aren't held, kissed, and nurtured, so Christians cannot grow if they are not lifted up, loved unconditionally, and encouraged.

When the apostle Paul entered Philippi, he had no idea that God would soon provide him with a community of fellow believers he would encourage, and be encouraged by, through their mutual faith. While no church or group of believers is perfect, when we follow the lead of God's Holy Spirit and trust in the principles we learn in the Bible, the Body of Christ is God's amazing provision of encouragement and support.

REVIEW OF DAY 1: GRACE AND PEACE (PHILIPPIANS 1:1–2)

Believers are also saints. Yes, we know we are not saints in the world's terminology (perfect and pious), but neither are we what we used to be (sinners in need of salvation). The New Testament addresses Christians not as sinners but as saints, or holy ones, because of our faith in Jesus Christ (1 Corinthians 6:11).

Dr. Ken Boa is a fellow saint and mentor of mine. He always ends his emails with, "Wishing you God's grace and peace." I used to take that phrase for granted, but after studying Paul's purpose in that statement, I see them differently. I'm reminded that it was the grace of God that allowed me to enter into and continue to experience the peace of God. It is God's grace that allows me to see myself as a saint. Dr. Boa describes the effects of grace in this way: "We are humbled but not degraded, while we are exalted but not inflated."

If God's grace neither degrades us nor inflates us, where does that leave us? How do you see yourself?

_____

_____

_____

_____

_____

_____

_____

What kind of impact should a life of grace and peace have on your relationship with others–Christians and non-Christians?
Christians:

_____

_____

_____

_____

Non-Christians:

_____

_____

_____

_____

REVIEW OF DAY 2: GRATITUDE AND AFFECTION (PHILIPPIANS 1:3–5)

The roots of some species of trees grow wide and yet not deep enough to keep the tree upright, but by intermingling with other tree roots of the same species, each individual tree is strengthened against windstorms. Strength in

> *Think of all the aspects of community by which Christians benefit from being the family of God in the Body of Christ:*
> *fellowship*
> *growth*
> *support*
> *friendship*
> *encouragement*
> *accountability*

numbers is a perfect picture of fellowship and Christian community. When we stand with one another and pray for one another, we can better resist the spiritual forces that come against us when we least expect them. Jesus said, "For where two or three come together in my name, there am I with them" (Matthew 18:19–20).

Describe the spiritual community you are part of–those you can call on to stand with you in a time of need. If you are not part of such a community, what do you think that would look like and how can you join one?

_____

_____

_____

_____

_____

REVIEW OF DAY 3: GOOD WORKS WITHIN (PHILIPPIANS 1:6–8)

There are some days I am not crazy about my own thoughts or behavior. On those days, I am reminded by Philippians 1:6 that God is not grading me. Rather, He is growing me into the image of Christ. He began a good work in me and will carry it on until it is complete on the day I see Christ face-to-face. He is doing the same with you, as you put your faith in Christ.

📖 Hebrews 12:2 uses two key words to describe Jesus as the one who began and who continues our process of transformation:

"Jesus is the _____ *and* _____ *of our faith."*

📖 On days you may not like your own thoughts or actions, how can Philippians 1:6 and Hebrews 12:2 help get your thoughts off of yourself and onto God?

_____

_____

_____

_____

It is easy as a Christian to feel discouraged, because we often fail in our attempt at holiness. But here's the truth: When we do good, it's because of God's grace. When we do badly, God's grace ensures that we will do better. God, by His Spirit and His Word, is constantly *"showing us truth, exposing our rebellion, correcting our mistakes,* [and] *training us to live God's* way" (2 Timothy 3:16, MSG). When we fail, He is there to pick us up, forgive us, and move us forward. This should give us confidence that we are changing and growing–that one day we will become all God has planned for us to be (Romans 8:28–29).

REVIEW OF DAY 4: GIFT OF PRAYER (PHILIPPIANS 1:9–11)

It's a double blessing when we see members of our immediate and extended families also become members of God's forever family. As parents, one of the most wonderful privileges we have is the opportunity to raise our children in the faith and nurture them toward their own decisions for Christ and to pray for them.

The prayer Paul prayed for the Philippians is a perfect prayer to pray for our children. What better gifts to pass on to our children than the gifts of love, knowledge, discernment, and purity?

Describe your current practice of prayer for your family, friends, church, and nation and ways you would like to see your prayer life change:

_____

_____

_____

_____

_____

Review Philippians 1:1–11

Review the Scriptures and content of this week's lessons and identify three ideas, themes, or action points that struck you from what you studied this week. Look for ideas to apply to your own life.

1. _____

_____

_____

_____

_____

2. _____

_____

_____

_____

3. _____

_____

_____

_____

Reflect on Philippians 1:6

> . . . being confident of this, that he who began a good work in you will carry it on to completion until the day of Christ Jesus.

What aspect of your life are you eager to see become more Christ-like?

_____

_____

_____

_____

_____

Remember God's Grace in Your Life

 Heavenly Father, Author and Perfecter of our faith, thank You for beginning a good work in me and promising to continue transforming my life until I meet Jesus face-to-face. Thank You for viewing me not as a sinner, but as a saint washed clean of all my sins and failures. Please grant me the grace to continue growing in love, discernment, and purity, that You may be glorified in my life. In Christ's name I pray. Amen.

Philippians 1:12-30

LESSON OVERVIEW
ENCOURAGEMENT THROUGH TRIALS

My daughter and I went to a wedding in the city where my mother, grandmother, and great-grandmother grew up. While there, I decided to give my daughter a tour of the graveyard at one of the churches where our ancestors were buried. We were amazed at how old the graves were. Some relatives were born in the 1700s and died in the early 1800s. We talked about how hard life was then. Children died young. Poverty was common, and war was familiar.

Yet we came across some encouraging words on the gravestone of one of our relatives. As we read them, we knew that no matter what trial he faced in life, this was a man who lived with hope. The inscription, excerpted from an old hymn by William Bathhurst, read:

> *Why should our tears in sorrow flow when God recalls his own;*
> *And bids them leave a world of woe for an immortal crown?*
> *Is not even death a gain to those whose life to God was given?*
> *Gladly to earth their eyes they close to open them in heaven.*

Paul suffered greatly during his life as well, yet found encouragement in the hope that he had a future life with the God who sustained him. Paul is reminding the Philippians that they have hope too. There would be no situation in their lives that Jesus could not control, even in the very end. That alone was great reason to rejoice.

CIRCUMSTANCES BRING OPPORTUNITY (PHILIPPIANS 1:12–18)

There is no circumstance in your life that God cannot take and work out for good. Paul's first imprisonment in Rome (A.D. 59–60) came about ten years after he started the church in Philippi (Acts 16:11–40). In his letter (Philippians 1:13–14), Paul makes clear reference to being "in chains," but he also goes on to explain how God was using his situation for the furtherance of the Gospel. For Paul, being in prison simply meant a different venue for exhibiting and proclaiming the grace of God in Christ.

Any circumstance Paul found himself in was an opportunity to bring glory to God.

A "CHAIN" REACTION

Now I want you to know, brothers, that what has happened to me has really served to advance the gospel. As a result, it has become clear throughout the whole palace guard and to everyone else that I am in chains for Christ. Because of my chains, most of the brothers in the Lord have been encouraged to speak the word of God more courageously and fearlessly. (Philippians 1:12–14)

One woman I've always admired is Susanna Wesley, wife of Samuel Wesley and the mother of John and Charles Wesley. She was the youngest of her parents' twenty-five children and gave birth to nineteen children, though nine of them died in infancy. Of the remaining ten, only eight of her children were still alive when she died. Her husband left her for a long time because times were hard and they were under financial strains. In the midst of her hardship and being "chained" to the house to raise her children, Susannah chose to bury herself in God's Word instead of burying herself in self-pity.

While she never preached a sermon or wrote a book, the ripple effect of teaching her children God's Word is astounding. She is known by many as the "Mother of Methodism," as it was her sons John and Charles who founded the Methodist movement. It is said that in order to have quiet time alone with God, Susanna Wesley would sit in a chair and pull her apron up and over her head, creating a sanctuary of peace amidst the distractions of a house full of small children.

I recently had the opportunity to visit the home and grave of Mrs. Wesley in England. In a nearby museum, some of the countless letters she wrote to her children, encouraging them in the faith, were on display. Like the Apostle Paul, Susanna was more concerned with the spread of God's Word than with the circumstances and difficulties of her own life. Just as she could never have anticipated how God would use those letters and her two sons, likewise Paul had no idea that his one letter to the Philippians would be read by millions for generations to come.

Next time you find yourself "chained" to an uncomfortable or undesirable set of circumstances, remember that God is not limited by your chains. He wants to use you, in spite of your circumstances, to demonstrate His power.

📖 In Philippians 1:13–14, what two benefits did Paul cite that arose from his imprisonment?

_____

_____

_____

_____

Describe a particularly limiting set of circumstances in your life right now. What is God showing you about how He wants to use your situation for His glory?

_____

_____

_____

AMBITION BECOMES ADVANTAGE

It is true that some preach Christ out of envy and rivalry, but others out of goodwill. The latter do so in love, knowing that I am put here for the defense of the gospel. The former preach Christ out of selfish ambition, not sincerely, supposing that they can stir up trouble for me while I am in chains. But what does it matter? The important thing is that in every way, whether from false motives or true, Christ is preached. And because of this I rejoice. Yes, and I will continue to rejoice. (Philippians 1:15–18)

God can use anyone for His purposes. And He uses unexpected circumstances or unexpected people to carry His message of hope into this dark world.

My husband and I visited Cuba in the 1980s on a business trip. The tightly controlled government provided a wonderful female interpreter and guide who showed us around Havana and other parts of the island nation. The conditions in the country were heartbreaking; we witnessed so many sad and hopeless looks on the faces of the people we met. When it was time to leave, many in our group offered our guide small gifts of appreciation for her service to us—a bracelet, scarf, and other gifts. I remembered I had a small New Testament pocket Bible in my purse, so I pulled our guide to the side and asked if she had ever read the Bible. She said she hadn't, but had heard of the Bible and had always wanted to read it. I gave her an English language New Testament but made one request: that she read and translate it into Spanish for others in her family and community. She said she would. Two years later, an individual from my husband's company returned from a follow-up trip to Cuba with a message for me. He had met the same guide, and she wanted him to convey a message to me about how her life had changed as a result of reading the New Testament I left with her and how she had read it to others as well. (I later learned she had managed to gain her freedom from the oppressive Communist regime after leaving Cuba.) All I could think of was Isaiah 55:11:

so is my word that goes out from my mouth:
It will not return to me empty,
but will accomplish what I desire
and achieve the purpose for which I sent it.

We never know what can be accomplished in the most limiting situations—
either ours or someone else's. If we will be faithful to look with spiritual
eyes, we will see what God wants to accomplish in and through us.

  Why was Paul able to rejoice at the same time he was a prisoner?
(Philippians 1:18)

_____

_____

_____

APPLY How difficult is it for you to believe God is at work when you are
in a difficult situation? Write Romans 8:28 in your own words.

_____

_____

_____

Responding to Scripture

How would you summarize the main theme or idea of Philippians 1:12–18?

_____

_____

_____

_____

Responding to Life

How should that idea impact your life today? What can you apply to your
own circumstances?

_____

_____

_____

_____

Responding to God

 Dear heavenly Father, thank You that You can
take bad things that happen and turn them into something good.
Please give me a heart for the Gospel like Paul's. I want to spread
Your Good News no matter what road I take or what difficult circumstance I encounter. Please use me for Your glory. May I see
every unexpected turn or every bump in the road as a way to get a
better glimpse of Your glory and Your purposes in this life. In the
mighty name of Jesus I pray. Amen.

COURAGE AND CONVICTION (PHILIPPIANS 1:19–20)

Paul was wrongfully imprisoned, yet he was able to rejoice in the midst of his trials. He knew that it is not what happens to us in life that is of prime importance, but how we respond to our circumstances. He found joy, not in imprisonment, but in the reality of his relationship with Christ in the midst of it. More than our words, our response to adversity reveals what we truly believe.

Paul also did not know that he would be released only to be imprisoned in Rome again later and that he would be martyred. But the details of what happened were less important than what Paul saw as his goal: to exalt Christ, whether in life or in death. He wanted to be wherever he could be of the greatest service to Christ and His Gospel. Throughout history, dedicated followers of Christ have viewed changing circumstances as nothing more than changing opportunities to see God's hand at work.

HIS GLORY THROUGH MY CIRCUMSTANCES

For I know that through your prayers and the help given by the Spirit of Jesus Christ, what has happened to me will turn out for my deliverance. (Philippians 1:19)

Each of us will face some time of difficulty in this life, during which hope appears to be lost. However, trials are not meant to reveal the absence of hope but the presence of Christ in you. Whatever circumstance or trial you find yourself in, the purpose is so "the life of Jesus may also be revealed in … [your] body" (2 Corinthians 4:10).

Corrie ten Boom was a Dutch Christian imprisoned in a German concentration camp during World War II. During her suffering, she vowed to God that if He allowed her to live she would go wherever He led her and tell everyone about the love and forgiveness of Christ. Miraculously, when the Nazis took her to prison, she was able to smuggle her small Bible past the guards as a result of prayer, and began holding Bible classes by candlelight for a growing group of believers. This group became known throughout the camp as "the crazy people where they have hope." After ten months of prison and the loss of her father and sister, Corrie was set free due to a clerical error the very week an order was given to kill the remaining women of her age in the camp.

Though Corrie could not understand why she had to suffer at the time, she realized later that God had used her to share the gift of salvation through Christ with so many before they lost their lives. Though they endured horrific conditions in prison and later died, they found ultimate freedom and life in Christ. Corrie went on to write nine books and travel all over the world, sharing Christ's message of forgiveness and hope in times of trouble. She wanted everyone to know that Jesus is the only true place of refuge in this world—the only hope that cannot be taken away. Like Paul, Corrie was more focused on the salvation of other lives than the discomfort of her own.

Did You Know?

CORRIE TEN BOOM

Corrie ten Boom (d. 1983), was born into a Christian family in Holland who helped many Jews escape the Nazi Holocaust during World War II. She followed her father in becoming a watchmaker and was a leader in the Dutch Reformed Church as a young person. Her later book, *The Hiding Place*, was a reference to a secret room built into the top floor of the ten Booms' residence where Jews could hide during searches by Nazi soldiers. The entire family was eventually arrested for their work in aiding the Jews.

Did You Know?

FOXE'S BOOK OF MARTYRS

The most famous record of Protestant Christians who suffered for their faith from the first through the sixteenth century is *The Book of Martyrs* by John Foxe. First published in English in 1563, the book was 1,800 large pages of text and woodcut illustrations. It went through several further editions and remains in print in an abridged format today.

Perhaps you are trapped in an emotional prison right now; you see no way to escape what feels like unbearable pressure. Due to aging or illness, your life on this earth may even be drawing to a close and fear is setting in. Now is your opportunity to join those "crazy people who have hope" because they know the one who is in charge of their outcome. The same Jesus who liberated Corrie ten Boom from a concentration camp can free you from whatever emotional or spiritual confinement you are experiencing.[4]

What two factors did Paul cite as being critical to his ultimate deliverance from prison? (Philippians 1:19)

1. _____

_____

2. _____

_____

📖 Based on Galatians 5:22–23, how have you seen "the Spirit of Jesus Christ" (the Holy Spirit) free you from an emotional or spiritual confinement?

_____

_____

_____

HIS GLORY THROUGH MY BODY

I eagerly expect and hope that I will in no way be ashamed, but will have sufficient courage so that now as always Christ will be exalted in my body, whether by life or by death. (Philippians 1:20)

A Christian high school football coach in southern Georgia has been in the news in our state in recent months. He had been praying for ways to demonstrate the reality of Christ to his football players; not long after, he was diagnosed with ALS, or Lou Gehrig's disease. This debilitating, fatal disease destroys the body's neuro-muscular capacity while leaving the mind intact. ALS leads to a slow, debilitating, and untimely death.

But Coach Jeremy Williams of Greenville High School, like the Apostle Paul, is taking every opportunity to spread his life message of faith in Christ. He was named National High School Football Coach of the Year in 2010 and was the subject of a season-long documentary film covering his team. Williams was reduced to coaching from a motorized wheelchair along the sidelines, but his players have rallied around him and his message of faith and perseverance through trials.

Coach Williams's body is gradually becoming his prison, but his Spirit-led voice has not been silenced. Indeed, the entire nation has directed its attention to the Georgia coach who rejoices in his spiritual life as his physical life slips away. Like Paul, Coach Williams's desire to spread the good news of Jesus Christ far outweighs his difficult circumstances. Just as Paul saw the Gospel being spread further due to his imprisonment (Philippians 1:15–18), so Coach Williams is watching good come from his illness.

Whether chained in prison or bound to a wheelchair—or tied up by some other circumstance—those filled with the Spirit of God continue to be the voice of God to those who lack hope in this world.

By his need for "courage" (Philippians 1:20), how did Paul present himself as a real person–not a "super saint"–in his trying circumstances? What was the source of his courage?

_____

_____

_____

Describe a situation in which God gave you a sense of joy in the midst of a trial:

_____

_____

_____

Can you say with Paul "whether by life or by death"? (Philippians 1:20) What would be the source of your courage (or lack of it)?

_____

_____

_____

_____

Responding to Scripture

What is Paul's big idea or main theme in Philippians 1:19–20?

_____

_____

_____

_____

Responding to Life

What would be the best way for you to integrate this theme into your own life today and in the future?

_____

_____

_____

_____

Responding to God

Heavenly Father, I don't know what the future holds for my life, but I trust You hold the future. I am not a courageous super-saint—just a Christian who wants to grow in faith and maturity and, yes, courage. I pray You will strengthen me through Your

"Courage is fear that has said its prayers."

Anonymous

"Take courage. We walk in the wilderness today and in the Promised Land tomorrow."

Dwight L. Moody

Word and by Your Holy Spirit, who lives in me. Please grant me the grace to be able to say that, whether in life or in death, my goal is to know Christ and to make him known to others. This I ask in his name. Amen.

Philippians 1:12-30

DAY THREE

CAUGHT IN THE MIDDLE (PHILIPPIANS 1:21–26)

Put Yourself in Their Shoes
HOW PAUL LIVED

Here are the ways Paul's life was threatened on a daily basis:

• Troubles, hardships, and distresses
• Beatings, imprisonments, and riots
• Hard work, sleepless nights, hunger, thirst and nakedness
• Dishonor and bad reports
• Accused of being a false apostle, a nobody
• Poverty
• Multiple exposures to death
• Being flogged on five different occasions
• Being beaten with rods three times
• Stoning
• Three ship-wrecks, adrift in the open sea
• Crossing dangerous rivers, escaping bandits
• Threatened by Jews, Gentiles, false Christians

From 2 Corinthians 6, 11

F ew of us face decisions like the Apostle Paul contemplated while in prison: the decision to live or die. It wasn't really his decision to make, of course. As a prisoner of Rome, he knew that humanly speaking, his life was in the emperor's hands. By expressing his "either/or" predicament the way he did, though, illustrates a truth that is central to the Christian experience: we don't cling to life because we fear death; we live so that others may live the life of Christ as well.

Paul thought that if he lost his life during his imprisonment in Rome, he would "depart to be with Christ." On the other hand, if he was released from prison, he would continue his ministry for those who didn't know Christ.

Paul lived his life fearlessly; he didn't fear living, nor did he seem to fear dying, because he knew he belonged to the One who lived and died fearlessly for him.

WHEN TO DIE IS GOD'S DECISION

For to me, to live is Christ and to die is gain. If I am to go on living in the body, this will mean fruitful labor for me. Yet what shall I choose? I do not know! I am torn between the two: I desire to depart and be with Christ, which is better by far; but it is more necessary for you that I remain in the body. (Philippians 1:21–24)

The Apostle Paul lived daily with the possibility of dying. The list of things he lived through included multiple shipwrecks, beatings, imprisonments, stoning, and attacks by bandits. The man had learned to hold life lightly (2 Corinthians 6:4–10, 11:23–29). He ended up in prison in Rome only because he was saved by Roman soldiers from death at the hands of a Jewish mob in Jerusalem some weeks before and demanded the opportunity to be heard by Caesar, his right as a Roman citizen (Acts 21:27–36, 25:10–12).

Paul lived life tenuously because he lived in a culture antagonistic toward the Gospel. He was a threat to the status quo of his day, and he knew it. Humanly speaking, he kissed the future good-bye every day when he started out, never knowing which day would be his last.

 How has God called you to stand against the status quo where you live? What do you think you would be willing to endure in order to accomplish His purposes in your life?

_____

_____

_____
_____
_____

📖 What did Paul say dying represented to him? What do his words, *"If I am to go on living . . ."* imply as to who was in charge of his death (Philippians 1:21–22)?

_____
_____
_____

The apostle Paul was aware daily of the thin line between life and death in his calling as an apostle, but most Christians don't think that way today. We set out at the beginning of every day, giving little or no thought to the nearness of death. On September 11, 2001, nearly three thousand people left home with the full expectation they would return safe and sound that night.

Whether we realize it or not, every person faces the dilemma Paul expressed—whether it is better to live or die. Most people would choose to live because they fear death. But Paul's passion for God and God's people is what drove his dilemma and kept him from the fear of dying. Why did Paul struggle with the decision between life and death (Philippians 1:22)?

_____
_____
_____

Using Paul's dilemma as a guide, write down why you would be hard-pressed to choose between life and death:

Advantage of Dying	Advantages of Living
1. _____	1. _____
2. _____	2. _____
3. _____	3. _____

Neither Paul nor we have to make that decision. The time and manner of our death is in God's hands (Psalm 139:16). But it is right for us to wrestle with the "what if?" factor. How comfortable are we with putting our life in God's hands? If God calls us home before we want to go, are we okay with that? Only Christians have a good reason to answer in the affirmative: to be absent from the body is to be at home with the Lord (2 Corinthians 5:8). When we die is in God's hands. But something else is totally in our hands: how we choose to live.

HOW TO LIVE IS OUR DECISION

Convinced of this, I know that I will remain, and I will continue with all of you for your progress and joy in the faith, so that through my being with you again your joy in Christ Jesus will overflow on account of me. (Philippians 1:25–26)

"Fear not that your life shall come to an end, but rather that it shall never have a beginning."

John Henry Newman

"Take care of your life and the Lord will take care of your death."

George Whitefield

Put Yourself in Their Shoes
PAUL'S DEATH

Nothing about the death of the apostle Paul is recorded in the New Testament. It is believed that he was put to death in Rome by Emperor Nero around A.D. 65-67, as was the Apostle Peter. Second Timothy was Paul's last epistle, written to Timothy from a dungeon in Rome before his martyrdom.

If God suddenly communicated with you and gave you the option of leaving earth and joining Christ in heaven right now, how would you respond? Paul wrote as if God was giving him that choice; he was using powerful words to show the tension between his passion and longing for Christ and his overwhelming desire to save as many on earth as possible. Choose heaven or stay on earth? It wasn't his choice, of course, but he pretended it was *so the Philippians would know how much he loved them and wanted to serve them in the future.* Paul was doing what we all should be doing: fulfilling our calling to live for Christ on earth until God calls us home. When Paul said, "I know that I will remain," (Philippians 1:25) he was saying, "As far as I know, it's God's will that I remain on earth." Why? *"For [the Philippians'] progress and joy in the faith."*

Usually Christians express a measure of hesitancy about going to heaven because there are so many things on earth they would still like to do: take a favorite trip, see their children get married, get that next promotion, or build their dream house. But I don't see anything like those reasons in Paul's letter. Paul had only one reason to remain on earth and that was to continue to help people "press on toward the goal to win the prize for which God has called … [them] heavenward in Christ Jesus" (Philippians 3:14).

God has *not* given us the responsibility for when we will die, but He *has* given us responsibility for how we will live and the impact we will have on others for Christ's sake. That much is our choice.

APPLY What did Paul want the Philippians to experience as a result of his continuing to minister to them (Philippians 1:26)? In whose life is the joy of the Lord overflowing today because God put you in his or her life?

_____

_____

_____

_____

Responding to Scripture

In one sentence or phrase, describe what you believe Paul's main idea to be in Philippians 1:21–26.

_____

_____

Responding to Life

How do you see this idea changing your life today? How can you apply what Paul wrote about?

_____

_____

_____

_____

_____

Heavenly Father, today, I submit myself again to Your plan for my life. As of this moment, I believe it is Your will for me to be on earth, carrying out my calling as a follower of Christ. Please help me to make Christ and his kingdom my primary reason for living. Help me share the joy of knowing Christ with those You put in my life. Please allow Your joy to overflow in me so it might overflow in others. In Christ's name. Amen.

Conduct That Is Worthy (Philippians 1:27–30)

Philippians 1:12-30

T here has been much discussion in the news lately about how Americans conduct themselves in wartime and how this behavior differs from the behavior of our parents and grandparents, since our "war on terror" is different from past wars. However the issue is settled, it acknowledges the reality that any country has certain expectations about how its citizens should behave—expectations that uphold the traditions of their culture (morally, socially, politically, and spiritually).

That was true in Paul's day as well. Philippi was part of the Roman Empire and as such, Philippians (whether Jew or Gentile) were Roman citizens. That status brought with it certain expectations that were enforced by the iron hand of Roman law. But Paul reminded the Philippians that they were to live by a higher standard. They were to live "in a manner worthy of the gospel of Christ" (Philippians 1:27). Just as a Philippian who lived like a barbarian would bring reproach upon Rome, so a Christian who lives in an un-Christ-like way will bring reproach on Christ and His Gospel.

The book of Job tells the story of Satan's temptation of Job in an attempt to embarrass or shame God when Job would, presumably, act in a manner unworthy of God (Job 1—2). When Job resisted the temptation to curse God, it was Satan, not God, who was embarrassed. When we walk as citizens of the kingdom of heaven (Ephesians 3:20, 4:1) we bring glory to Jesus Christ, our King. Anything less on our part is a lifestyle unworthy of the gospel of Christ.

UNITED FOR THE GOSPEL

> *Whatever happens, conduct yourselves in a manner worthy of the gospel of Christ. Then, whether I come and see you or only hear about you in my absence, I will know that you stand firm in one spirit, contending as one man for the faith of the gospel without being frightened in any way by those who oppose you. This is a sign to them that they will be destroyed, but that you will be saved—and that by God. (Philippians 1:27–28)*

Word Study
CONDUCT

The verb Paul used for "conduct yourselves" (Philippians 1:27) is *politeuomai*, which is connected to the Greek words *polis* (city) and *polites* (citizen), and is connected to our word "politics." Summarizing those shared words, "conduct yourself" means to act in accordance with expected norms of the city (kingdom) in which you reside.

Like most young mothers, I can remember sending my children off to elementary school with admonitions to be good, do their best, be sweet, work hard, and all the rest. I'm sure my motives were mixed. I certainly wanted them to develop and display character traits that would stay with them for a lifetime, but I also didn't want them to tarnish the McGuirk name. That is, I didn't want them to embarrass me. When we send our children out into the world, we're sending our good name and reputation along with them.

Paul may have felt a bit of that parental anxiety with the churches he planted all over the Mediterranean world. For instance, he was particularly exasperated with the Corinthian church on several counts: jealousy and quarreling, believers suing each other, immorality, turning the Lord's Table into a carnal feast (1 Corinthians 1:11; 3:1; 5:1; 6:1; 11:17). Their behavior was no different from the non-believers who were supposed to be seeing Jesus through them.

With the Philippians, Paul's concerns were different. The believers in Philippi were being opposed by other citizens. Remember, Paul and Silas were severely beaten and thrown into jail because they cast a demon out of a fortune teller (Acts 16:16). Paul was afraid that such opposition might crack the unity of the believers. He wanted them to stand together and thereby strengthen each other. Paul is writing this letter from jail about ten years after the events of Acts 16 in Philippi, so it's likely that when believers from Philippi visited Paul in Rome, they brought word to Paul of the ongoing opposition in their area and the toll it was taking on the unity of the church.

How did Paul want the believers in Philippi to "contend" for the Gospel? If they failed to remain unified, how would that reflect on the value of the Gospel in the eyes of observers in Philippi (Philippians 1:27–28) ?

_____

_____

_____

_____

There is a purpose for godly behavior. How does Paul explain the two-fold reason for our walking in a manner that is worthy of the Gospel (Philippians 1:28b) ?

1. What it says about us: _____

2. What it says about others: _____

It is sad to say, but too often there is little behavioral difference between Christians and non-Christians. Non-Christians say by their behavior that they don't believe Christ died and was resurrected for them. But when we live the way they live, our lives say the same thing. Paul was hard on himself for the same reason; he didn't want his life to negate the power of the message he was giving his life to deliver (1 Corinthians 9:27).

In the face of opposition to the Gospel, what does it mean to live "in a manner worthy of the gospel of Christ" (Philippians 1:27) ?

_____

_____

Put Yourself in Their Shoes

CHRISTIAN BEHAVIOR

Paul's emphasis on "conduct" should not be confused with legalism, or trying to earn one's salvation on the basis of behavior or works. In the Old Testament, the Law represented an externally imposed set of behavioral standards designed to expose man's lack of internal spiritual strength and lead him to Christ (Galatians 3:24). In the New Testament, Christian conduct is evidence of a new internal reality—Jesus Christ living out His life through the believer (Galatians 2:21). When we fail to allow the Holy Spirit to manifest Christ's life through us, we call into question our profession of belonging to Him—and dishonor the life He lived and the death He suffered to make it possible for us to live a life pleasing to God.

_____

_____

SUFFERING FOR THE GOSPEL

For it has been granted to you on behalf of Christ not only to believe on him, but also to suffer for him, since you are going through the same struggle you saw I had, and now hear that I still have. (Philippians 1:29–30)

I've heard many young or spiritually immature Christians express surprise when they experience trouble or pain. Some even give up following Jesus because of their problems. For some reason, they think believing in Jesus comes with a Get-Out-of-Trouble-Free card for the rest of their lives. The truth is, Jesus told His disciples, "In this world you will have trouble" (John 16:33).

What did Paul tell the Philippians they had been granted in addition to their belief in Christ (Philippians 1:29)?

_____

_____

Paul reminded the Philippians (Philippians 1:30) of what he experienced in Philippi and mentioned his current imprisonment in Rome—all for the sake of the Gospel of Christ.

📖 Read Matthew 10:22 on suffering as a Christian. What is the principle here that tells us to expect to suffer for Jesus in this world?

_____

_____

_____

Responding to Scripture

What is the big idea Paul conveys to the Philippians in Philippians 1:27–30? How do you think he would suggest you accomplish this?

_____

_____

_____

_____

Responding to Life

How might you best apply the message to walk worthy in the face of suffering for the Gospel of Christ?

_____

_____

_____

_____

_____

_____

> "The staying power of our faith is neither demonstrated nor developed until it is tested by suffering."
>
> ## D. A. Carson

Heavenly Father, I truly do not want to bring shame or dishonor to the name of Your Son, especially when I'm opposed or suffer criticism for being a believer in Him. I pray for strength and grace to conduct myself in a manner worthy of the one who suffered so much for my sake. Please give me courage, strength, and unity with other believers so I may stand firm in my faith. Please let me live a life that will proclaim I'm not the same person I once was—that I've been granted the gift of salvation and the privilege of identifying with the sufferings of Christ. In his name I pray. Amen.

Philippians 1:12-30

DAY FIVE

Word Study
COURAGE

When we encourage someone, we instill courage in them—strength to carry on. The primary verb for "encourage" in the New Testament is *parakaleo*, which means "called along side of." From this verb comes *parakletos*, the word used by Jesus to describe the Holy Spirit (John 14:16, 26), translated "Counselor." When we meet with a counselor it is to gain courage and strength. When the Holy Spirit (Counselor) comes alongside us, it is to impart the same thing.

REVIEW FOR FOLLOWING GOD

When the church at Philippi sent Epaphroditus to Rome to deliver a gift to the imprisoned apostle, it's likely they felt sorry for him. That's understandable. We would feel badly for anyone who was imprisoned unjustly. But Paul didn't feel sorry for himself; he didn't look at the situation as a glass half empty. Paul saw the Gospel being preached by some who capitalized on his incarceration. Even though their motives were impure, Paul rejoiced that the Gospel was being proclaimed. He knew God was at work in every situation.

REVIEW OF DAY 1: CIRCUMSTANCES BRING OPPORTUNITY (PHILIPPIANS 1:12–18)

My husband Terry is an avid golfer and is often invited to out-of-town golf outings. These trips give me undisturbed time to work on my writing and ministry projects while he is on the golf course. On one of our trips, a dinner had been arranged for all the couples. I planned to skip it to continue working. But Terry wanted me to go with him, so I agreed.

I was seated next to a man with whom I chatted throughout dinner. As we talked, I learned that he didn't believe in God and would be mad at God even if He did exist. He had lost a teenage son in a tragic accident and had never gotten over it. As we talked, I prayed silently for the right words to encourage him to open his heart to God's love. By the end of the evening, the man had promised me he would go home, get on his knees, and ask God to show him who Jesus Christ really is. As my husband and I were preparing to leave the dinner, the man's wife (who had been seated on the other side of the table) stopped me to say what an answer to prayer the evening had been for her husband to open himself to the claims of Jesus.

I went home that night humbled by how God had used the evening. To think I almost missed out on a glorious encounter because I thought staying home to work on my bible study materials was more "spiritual." Whether in jail or on a golf outing, God can spread the Gospel through us when we least expect it.

APPLY Describe an example of how God used you to impact the life of another person, either by sharing the Gospel or the love of Christ, at a time you least expected.

_____

_____

_____

_____

REVIEW OF DAY 2: COURAGE AND CONVICTION (PHILIPPIANS 1:19–20)

The Apostle Paul was nothing if not a man of conviction, courage, and confidence. Even when he faced the possibility of death while confined to a jail in Rome, his faith never wavered.

God asked me to face the reality of death as I watched both my parents die of debilitating diseases within three months of one another. My father had ALS (Lou Gehrig's disease), and my mother had Alzheimer's disease. My father's body wasted away while his brain remained healthy; my mother's situation was the opposite—healthy body but deteriorating brain. To see both my parents decline rapidly at the same time challenged the faith of our family. My father was a model of grace under fire, as he lived daily with the inevitable outcome of an incurable disease. I was grateful my mother's Alzheimer's shielded her from awareness of my father's situation as well as her own declining state.

Whether by our own possible deaths or extreme difficulties, as with Paul or that of our loved ones, our faith can be put to the test. We are called to have courage, confidence, and conviction that God is in control, that this world is not our home, and that all things work together for good to those who love Him.

📖 Explain how Romans 8:28–29 has been the basis for your own courage in a past or present circumstance. Paul identifies God's "purpose" in Romans 8:29. What is it?

_____

_____

_____

_____

REVIEW OF DAY 3: CAUGHT IN THE MIDDLE (PHILIPPIANS 1:21–26)

Researching family trees is an increasingly popular hobby, and I must confess that I, too, have been drawn into this. Looking over my own family tree recently with names and dates stretching back to 1100 A.D. made me realize that each name represents a life that stretched over decades. For most of those names, all I know about them are the dates of their births and deaths and whom they married. Yet God knows every detail of each of their lives as He knows every detail of ours.

I also thought about the Apostle Paul. For him, living and dying were equal blessings. To live meant service for Christ; to die meant living with Christ forever. He had no anxiety about living or dying. In either case, his life was focused on eternity, either laying up treasures in heaven while on earth or enjoying those treasures when he arrived there.

Every Christian lives with the tension between present and future; the desire to make a difference for Christ now that will last for eternity; and the desire to leave the timetable to God and live every moment focused on Christ and eternity.

APPLY What choices or sacrifices have you made to keep your life focused on eternity? What investments of your time, talent, and treasure are you confident will have eternal consequences?

_____

_____

_____

_____

_____

REVIEW OF DAY 4: CONDUCT THAT IS WORTHY (PHILIPPIANS 1:27–30)

There is a paradox in the Christian life: We know we are not worthy of the grace of God extended to us through Christ (Mark 1:7; 1 Corinthians 15:9), yet we are told to "conduct [ourselves] in a manner worthy of the gospel of Christ" (Philippians 1:27). How do we know if we are "walking worthy?"

Maybe the home is the best starting point, since that's where our true self comes out. I once asked my husband and children to help me with a survey—ten questions on how I was doing as a _Christian_ wife and mother. I assured them I would not hold their answers against them, that I wanted them to be completely honest with their ratings. Though my husband tried to plead the Fifth to avoid incriminating himself, he finally decided I was serious and agreed to participate. Their ratings were eye-opening to me. I saw some areas in which I was not "walking worthy" of my relationship with Jesus and where I could improve. Not every woman wants to subject herself to a survey like I did, but talking with your family honestly and openly about how well your walk matches your talk could be eye-opening for you too.

I'm so glad God sees not only our actions but our motivations. He is ready to forgive us when we fail and empower us to walk in an increasingly worthy way. We are only able to walk worthy because he who walked perfectly lives in us (Galatians 2:20).

APPLY How do you balance the unworthy-worthy tension in your life? What helps you walk in a way that's worthy of Christ? What do you do when you don't?

_____

_____

_____

_____

_____

_____

> _"Only one life, yes only one,_
> _Now let me say,_
> _'Thy will be done;'_
> _And when at last_
> _I'll hear the call,_
> _I know I'll say, 'Twas worth it all.'_
> _Only one life, 'twill soon be past,_
> _Only what's done for Christ will last."_
>
> **C. T. Studd**

> _God does not justify us because we are worthy, but justifying makes us worthy._
>
> **Thomas Watson**

REVIEW PHILIPPIANS 1:12–30

Review the Scriptures and content of this week's lessons and identify three ideas, themes, or action points that struck you from what you studied this week. Especially look for ideas to apply to your own life.

1. _____
_____
_____
_____
_____

2. _____
_____
_____
_____
_____

3. _____
_____
_____
_____
_____

Reflect on Philippians 1:21

For to me, to live is Christ and to die is gain.

APPLY What changes do you need to make to become equally ready to die for Christ as to live for Christ?

_____
_____
_____
_____
_____
_____
_____

REMEMBER GOD'S GRACE IN YOUR LIFE

 Heavenly Father, please help me to see every situation and circumstance as an opportunity to proclaim the Gospel. Give me courage and conviction, even in the face of death and difficulty. Thank You that I do not have to fear death and that for me to live is Christ and to die is gain. Please show me the areas of my life where my character is less than my calling in You. I want to live for Jesus in every moment of my life. In Christ's name I pray. Amen.

Notes

Philippians 2:1-30

LESSON OVERVIEW

EXAMPLES OF HUMILITY

It has been almost a decade, yet I still remember his sermon like it was yesterday. It was Mother's Day, and I was scurrying around trying to get my four young children dressed and ready for church. As they and my husband finally made their way to the car, I sensed my frustration building. After all, this was Mother's Day!

As I sat there in the pew, the proud mom of my four little well-dressed ducklings, our pastor, Dr. Vic Pentz, told a story about a mom who, by all appearances, was a complete mess. She was poor, disheveled, disorganized (her house was a wreck), and her children were not exactly well-behaved. She had none of the qualities I thought of at the time as a mom who has it all together. Other mothers in the neighborhood secretly made fun of this woman, her many children, and her disorganized home. But her children saw their mom differently. They remembered her as a mother who loved them and was *always praying for them*. They had memories of her staring out the kitchen window each day, slowly washing dishes while praying for each one of them.

In time, those children became outstanding citizens who gave back to the community. They all excelled in school, received scholarships to top universities, became outstanding professionals in their fields, and most importantly, became men and women of faith. They attributed their success to their humble mother who truly had her priorities right. She was completely dependent on God for the future of her children.

God gave me a humbling message that day. I needed to be less concerned about my children's appearance and more concerned about praying for God's grace to be at work in their hearts. I was reminded to make sure I kept love and prayer at the top of my priority list for my children.

God humbles us because he loves us. On that Mother's Day, he gave me the right message at the right time. Now Paul is giving the Philippians the right message—to humble themselves in order to learn from Christ as well.

Philippians 2:1-30

DAY ONE

Word Study
FELLOWSHIP WITH THE SPIRIT

The Greek word for fellowship is *koinonia*, which is derived from the word *koinos* and means "common." Something held in common was something shared. If we have fellowship with another, it means we have something in common; or, we are one with them. Therefore, fellowship with the Spirit is to be one with Him; to be in partnership with Him.

CHRIST (PHILIPPIANS 2:1–11)

Chapter 2 of Philippians addresses the "how" of the Christian life. We find that Jesus Christ is our primary example, and since humility and Christ-like love do not come naturally to most of us, how do we live like Him? In truth, we can't live like Him in our own strength or by our own abilities. Our life can only resemble His when we dig in and so abide in Him that we begin to see His life through us, even to our surprise, as Paul describes in Galatians 2:20a: "I have been crucified with Christ and I no longer live, but Christ lives in me."

When my son was in junior high and high school, we sent him and his sisters to a Christian camp during the summer. Terry was the quiet one, which would be expected when you are a boy surrounded by three sisters, but he was an avid reader and very bright. Naturally, we hoped our children would learn about Jesus and understand the Gospel as they studied the Bible during that camp each summer.

One summer, when as I was attending the Parents' Night at the camp, I heard Terry was to receive an award—something about "third place." I did not give this much thought until the award was announced. It was actually called the "I'm Third" Award and the most coveted award at the camp. It was for the child who seemed most likely to put God first, others second, and himself third. I sat in tears as I watched him receive this recognition. Not only had he learned about Jesus, but more importantly, he had spent so much time with Jesus that he had begun to follow in His footsteps of humility.

Christ lives in us by the presence of the Holy Spirit. So only by being "filled with the Spirit" (Ephesians 5:18) can our life resemble the life of Christ. If you are a born-again believer (John 3:3–8), the Holy Spirit lives within you (Acts 2:38). If you are unsure about your relationship with Him, prayerfully ask Christ to forgive the past that made you the center of your life and empower your future with Him at the center. Then, as you try to live your life by faith, the indwelling Spirit of Christ will begin to guide and counsel you; you will see the promise of Philippians 1:6 fulfilled in your life: ". . . he who began a good work in you will carry it on to completion until the day of Christ Jesus."

BE A SERVANT TO OTHERS

If you have any encouragement from being united with Christ, if any comfort from his love, if any fellowship with the Spirit, if any tenderness and compassion, then make my joy complete by being like-minded, having the same love, being one in spirit and purpose. Do nothing out of selfish ambition or vain conceit, but in humility consider others better than yourselves. Each of you should look not only to your own interests, but also to the interests of others. (Philippians 2:1–4)

Once we are united by faith to Christ, Paul says certain things ought to be true of us. We, and other Christians, ought to be like-minded, exhibit Christ's love, and be one "in spirit and purpose." We don't know how others might act, but we can certainly take responsibility for our own Christ-likeness by being loving to others and seeking to fulfill Christ's Spirit and purpose for His church. When we do that, our lives will look distinctly different from the natural, carnal life that we lived before. Indeed, just as Christ came not to be served but to serve others (Mark 10:45), so we will do the same: become servants of others.

Paul wrote in Romans 8:4–5 that those who belong to Christ "do not live according to the sinful nature but according to the Spirit. Those who live according to the sinful nature have their minds set on what that nature desires; but those who live in accordance with the Spirit have their minds set on what the Spirit desires." The Holy Spirit, who dwells in us, accounts for the new desire we have to set our minds on the things of Christ. As Christ was devoted to serving others, so we will be devoted to serving Him by serving others as well and will feel fulfilled when we do so. We will fulfill Paul's admonition in Romans 12:10, "Be devoted to one another in brotherly love. Honor one another above yourselves."

📖 How does Philippians 2:4 expand the range of our concerns once we become Christians?

_____

_____

_____

_____

What do the words "devoted" and "honor" suggest to you about how relationships change after becoming a Christian?

_____

_____

_____

_____

BE A SERVANT LIKE CHRIST

Your attitude should be the same as that of Christ Jesus: Who, being in very nature God, did not consider equality with God something to be grasped, but made himself nothing, taking the very nature of a servant, being made in human likeness. And being found in appearance as a man, he humbled himself and became obedient to death—even death on a cross! Therefore God exalted him to the highest place and gave him the name that is above every name, that at the name of Jesus every knee should bow, in heaven and on earth and under the earth, and every tongue confess that Jesus Christ is Lord, to the glory of God the Father. (Philippians 2:5–11)

The Jews did not recognize Jesus when he came, because they were looking for a kingly Messiah, not a suffering servant. They weren't totally wrong in their expectations since the Old Testament does picture the Messiah coming

Word Study
"IF YOU HAVE ..."

In Philippians 2:1, Paul uses a Greek grammatical construction four times ("If . . . if . . . if . . . if . . . .") that implies an affirmative answer: "If you have any encouragement . . . comfort . . . fellowship . . . tenderness and compassion [and yes, you do] then . . . ." Since we have all these things, we should exemplify like-mindedness, humility, and care.

Put Yourself in Their Shoes
CHRISTLIKE

The original apostles understood the need to be like Christ, who made himself a servant. Paul (Romans 1:1; Galatians 1:10), James (James 1:1), Peter (2 Peter 1:1), Jude (Jude 1:1), and John (Revelation 1:1) all identified themselves as servants of Christ.

_____

Responding to Life

What can you do today and for the long-term to apply that theme to your life?

_____

_____

_____

_____

Responding to God

 Heavenly Father, I thank You that Jesus Christ was willing to humble Himself and submit Himself to Your will in order that my sins could be forgiven through His death on the cross. I pray You will allow Jesus' thought processes to be in me, as I yield myself to the Spirit who lives in me. I also pray You would give me the servant heart of Christ so that I would not seek to be served, but to serve others. Please help me to stay focused on Christ, not on myself. I pray in His name. Amen.

PAUL (PHILIPPIANS 2:12–18)

Too often, Christians think of humility as something it's not. We think humility is simply a gentler and kinder version of our self. But this is false humility, because it's still focused on self. This false humility can become a form of weakness—a willingness to compromise in order not to make waves or cause problems. But an unwillingness to be bold is not humility. Christ made waves and caused problems, yet we know he was humbled (Philippians 2:8). We can discern then that humility is not measured by quietness or conformity. Judging by Christ's life, humility is a willingness to set aside our own interests and doggedly pursue the interests of God. As C. S. Lewis so well put it, "Humility is not thinking less of yourself, but thinking of yourself less."

The apostle Paul mirrored Christ's humility demonstrated by a lack of self-concern. After realizing it was Jesus who confronted him on the road to Damascus, Paul's first words were, *"What shall I do, Lord?"* (See Acts 22:10a.) Thus began a new life of humility for Paul. His focus shifted from what he wanted to what the Lord wanted. A perfect example of Paul's humility was his three-time plea for God to remove the *"thorn in* [his] *flesh"* (2 Corinthians 12:7–10), something God allowed in his life for the express purpose of keeping him humble. Paul wanted the thorn removed, but when

"It is very difficult to be humble if you are always successful, so God chastises us with failure at times in order to humble us, to keep us in a state of humility."

D. Martyn Lloyd-Jones

Philippians 2:1–30

DAY TWO

"Humility is the beginning of true intelligence."

John Calvin

> "A blossom is the beginning of fruit bearing, and submission, the beginning of humility."
>
> Unknown

> "If an experience fails to engender humility, charity, mortification, holy simplicity, and silence . . . of what value is it?"
>
> St. John of the Cross

God said no, Paul submitted humbly to that response. Paul accepted the truth that the grace of God was somehow sufficient. And even though God refused to deliver him from this trouble, it would be used to draw him into closer union and fellowship with the one who suffered all things for us.

Biblical humility is not passive. It takes courage and is not for the timid or faint of heart. The goal of the humble Christian is to carry out whatever God wants to happen on earth. True humility is found in us when we are dead to self and alive in Christ; when we can say with John the Baptist, "He must become greater; I must become less" (John 3:30), and when our eyes are fixed "on Jesus, the author and perfecter of our faith" (Hebrews 12:2).

HUMBLY WORK OUT YOUR SALVATION

> *Therefore, my dear friends, as you have always obeyed—not only in my presence, but now much more in my absence—continue to work out your salvation with fear and trembling, for it is God who works in you to will and to act according to his good purpose. (Philippians 2:12–13)*

The phrase "work out your salvation" seems confusing, even contradictory. Aren't we saved already? What is there to "work out"? Doesn't our salvation come as a gift of grace, "not by works, so that no one can boast" (Ephesians 2:9)? The answer to all three questions is yes. By "work out," Paul means putting our salvation into practice, making our salvation practical and provable to all who hear our claim to be saved. Immediately after declaring that our salvation is a gift of grace, Paul says, "For we are God's workmanship, created in Christ Jesus to do good works" (Ephesians 2:10a). Salvation from sin is *His* work in me, and *my* work is walking in those good works He has planned for me—the ones "God prepared in advance for us to do" (Ephesians 2:10b).

Even though this "work" is our responsibility, it can only be accomplished through the enabling of the Holy Spirit. God's grace not only saves us but strengthens us to do His will. Even the Apostle Paul struggled with being consistently obedient when he tried in his own strength to work out his salvation. He wrote, "I do not understand what I do. For what I want to do I do not do, but what I hate I do. . . . For I have the desire to do what is good, but I cannot carry it out" (Romans 7:15, 18b). He concludes that only "Jesus Christ our Lord" can free him from failure and propel him toward a righteous life (Romans 7:24–25a).

Paul's experience is a reflection of true humility, admitting that on our own, we are helpless and hopeless to live a life pleasing to God. But by taking the focus off of our efforts and focusing on Christ, we are able to work out our salvation "by deeds done in that humility that comes from wisdom" (James 3:13).

APPLY How does popular culture encourage you to focus on self instead of on Christ?

_____

_____

_____

_____

What can help you the most to stay focused on Christ instead of trying to "act humble"?

_____

_____

_____

HUMBLY SHINE LIKE STARS

Do everything without complaining or arguing, so that you may become blameless and pure, children of God without fault in a crooked and depraved generation, in which you shine like stars in the universe as you hold out the word of life—in order that I may boast on the day of Christ that I did not run or labor for nothing. But even if I am being poured out like a drink offering on the sacrifice and service coming from your faith, I am glad and rejoice with all of you. So you too should be glad and rejoice with me. (Philippians 2:14–18)

A transformed life is a great witness to the power of Christ and becomes a shining light in a dark world. The Bible consistently speaks of the world as a "dark" place. Both the living Word (Jesus) and the written Word of God are pictured as lights shining in the darkness (John 1:5; 2 Peter 1:19). We ourselves were *"rescued from the dominion of darkness and brought . . . into the kingdom of the Son"* (Colossians 1:13). Therefore, to spread the light of truth, Jesus said that we are to *"let [our] light shine before men, that they may see [our] good deeds and praise [our] Father in heaven"* (Matthew 5:16).

Benjamin Franklin wrote in his autobiography about how dark the streets of Philadelphia were when he was a resident there. People were afraid to leave their homes at night because of crime. Franklin, typical of his inventive ways, proposed that every citizen be responsible for lighting the portion of the street in front of his home—the "homes" being row houses situated right next to one another. The effect of lighting each part would be to light entire streets of the city.

But the citizens failed to respond. Undeterred, Franklin put an oil lantern on a pole in front of his own residence each night. Like moths to a candle, people gravitated to the light and the safety it provided. When they experienced the benefit of Franklin's streetlight, others began to put lights in front of their houses. Soon, the streets of Philadelphia were transformed from darkness into light. Illumination and safety replaced darkness and fear.[5]

God intends for Christians to "shine like stars in the universe" as citizens of the kingdom of light in a dark world. Those in darkness are to find safety and security in us because of the light of God shining through us on our streets, in the neighborhood, at work, in school, and in our families.

 In what domain of your life is the need for spiritual light the greatest? To what degree are you shining as a light for Christ? What responses are you seeing? [Use a separate sheet if necessary.]

_____

_____

_____

"*The main evidence that we are growing in Christ is not exhilarating prayer experiences, but steadily increasing, humble love for other people.*"

Frederica Mathewes-Green

Put Yourself in Their Shoes

CROOKED AND DEPRAVED

Sin doesn't just happen in our lives; it has a pattern that first unfolded in Genesis 3:1-6: Whatever distracts us away from God is the first step, and it will invariably lead to doubting God's word, just as Eve doubted after being distracted by Satan. Doubt leads to the debate that goes on in our heads: "Did God really say...?" or "The Lord said . . . !" We will always be given the opportunity to choose whom we will believe, but debate will always leave us ripe for deception. If we choose the Enemy's lie over God's truth, desire will pave the rest of the way to sin, which we'll embrace, ingest into our lives, and even share with another, just like Eve did in Genesis 3:6. In what ways can you relate to this pattern?

Responding to Scripture

How would you describe Paul's main idea in Philippians 2:12–18?

_____

_____

_____

_____

_____

Responding to Life

How can you apply that idea in your life now? What benefits would result?

_____

_____

_____

_____

Responding to God

 Heavenly Father, I thank You for rescuing me from the kingdom of darkness and making me a citizen of your kingdom of light. I ask You to open my eyes to anything that might block the light of Christ and Your Word from shining forth clearly and humbly through me. I truly want light to overcome darkness in my life so others might find the salvation and security of Jesus through me. In his name I pray. Amen.

Philippians 2:1-30

DAY THREE

"The whole trouble in life is a concern about self."

D. Martyn Lloyd-Jones

TIMOTHY (PHILIPPIANS 2:19–24)

When I was a relatively new Christian, I was asked to teach a Sunday school class in my church. I eagerly accepted and prepared with great enthusiasm and hard work. As I walked into the room on the appointed day, my heart sank. Sitting in the class was the pillar of our church—the widow of our church's first pastor. At that time, Martha was in her late 90s and had spent more than half a century faithfully teaching the Bible to members of our church. When I rose to begin the lesson, I could hardly speak. I was so nervous. I made a joking reference to the obvious: a first-time teacher teaching the Teacher of Teachers!

In her typically humble way, Martha said, "Nancy, go ahead. You are our teacher today, and we are eager to hear what you have to say." Needless to say, my entire lesson consisted of calling on Martha to address the various topics we discussed so that, without knowing it, she appropriately ended up teaching the class.

Deferring to Martha was not humility on my part. It was more an act of survival. But Martha deferring to me was certainly humility. She wasn't interested in promoting herself as the authority but rather was more concerned about supporting a rookie teacher who needed encouragement and even room to fail if needed. Though she was in her 90s, Martha did what Timothy did: she took an interest in the welfare of another person rather than exalting herself. Yes, I was the official teacher that day, but unofficially, I was the student at the feet of another humble servant of Christ.

Another student who followed a humble servant of Christ was Timothy. Paul probably met Timothy on his first missionary journey, when he and Silas passed through Lystra, the young man's hometown (Acts 14:6). Timothy was invited to join Paul and Silas on Paul's second journey when they passed through Lystra again (Acts 16:1). Timothy, born to a Gentile (Greek) father and a Jewish mother, was brought up in the faith by his mother and grandmother (2 Timothy 1:5). Young Timothy had grown into a respected disciple, and "The brothers at Lystra and Iconium spoke well of him" (Acts 16:2). Timothy became Paul's protégé in the faith and his most trusted supporter right up to the end of Paul's life (Philippians 2:19–24; 2 Timothy 4:9, 21). Paul made Timothy the pastor of the church at Ephesus and wrote two letters to him to encourage him in his pastoral duties there. The trait that distinguished Timothy and made him a model of humility was that he looked out for the interests of Jesus Christ and not for his own (Philippians 2:21). In that regard, he was like Jesus, like Paul, and like my sweet friend, Martha, submitting himself to the will of God.

TAKING AN INTEREST IN OTHERS

> *I hope in the Lord Jesus to send Timothy to you soon, that I also may be cheered when I receive news about you. I have no one else like him, who takes a genuine interest in your welfare. For everyone looks out for his own interests, not those of Jesus Christ. (Philippians 2:19–21)*

We saw on Day 1 of this week what Paul wrote to the Philippians about concern for others (Philippians 2:3). I love the way Eugene Peterson paraphrases this verse in *The Message*: "Don't push your way to the front; don't sweet-talk your way to the top. Put yourself aside, and help others get ahead." Then Paul gives the Philippians a living, breathing example of such a person: Timothy. Young Timothy was unique in the way he took an interest in the Philippians' welfare. "I have no one else like him," Paul wrote (Philippians 2:20).

Timothy also was unique in his ultimate commitment. While everyone else looked out for their own interests, Timothy looked out for the interests of Jesus Christ.

This should cause us to evaluate who we are and how we respond to others' requests for help. Are we willing to leave our workday or our homes to travel some distance to meet a need? Are we more likely to jump at the opportunity to serve someone, or are we more likely to find an excuse? Our attitude will determine everything when we are given opportunities to serve. If we see them as opportunities, chances to honor and serve the Lord, we are likely to go and find joy in our service. If we see them as obligations, there will be no joy in doing them.

This is an especially challenging concept to all of us in our various realms of leadership; everybody leads somebody, whether in the family, at church, or

Word Study
TIMOTHY

The Greek name "Timothy" was made of two Greek words: *time* (honor) and *theos* (God). Joined together they produce "Timothy," which meant "honoring God." This name is no doubt a reflection of the faith of Timothy's mother and grandmother, who were apparently Jewish believers in the Messiah-Jesus (2 Timothy 1:5).

Word Study
BEING CONCERNED

In Philippians 4:6 the Apostle Paul says that Christians should be anxious for nothing. But there is one thing we apparently should be anxious for: the welfare of others. The word "anxious" in Philippians 4:6 is translated from the same Greek word (*merimna*) translated "concern" or "genuine interest" in Philippians 2:20. Being fearfully anxious is one thing; being lovingly concerned is another. At the heart of both is care.

other venues. Whose interests are we looking out for the most: ours or our Lord's? It's easy to get deceived into thinking we should promote our interests or opinions or agendas, especially when it's something we feel passionate about, instead of those of Christ. Timothy apparently had not fallen prey to that temptation and remained a humble servant of Christ and His chief apostle, Paul.

 APPLY Whose welfare has God given you the opportunity to look out for? How aware are they of your concern for them?

_____

_____

_____

_____

_____

TRAINED TO SERVE OTHERS

But you know that Timothy has proved himself, because as a son with his father he has served with me in the work of the gospel. I hope, therefore, to send him as soon as I see how things go with me. And I am confident in the Lord that I myself will come soon. (Philippians 2:22–24)

When I read a biography of the late Mother Teresa, I was struck by something that characterized her childhood. When Agnes (her given name) was a young girl, she would accompany her mother around their neighborhood in their Albanian town as she checked on the welfare of their neighbors and met the needs of the poor. Her mother would often bring the poor to their home to care for them, feed them, and pray for them. Agnes absorbed and internalized all of this as a young girl as her mother informally mentored her daughter. By age twelve, she knew she wanted to live a religious life, meeting the needs of others. Then at age eighteen, she left home to enter training as a missionary nun. She never saw her family again.

It should come as no surprise to find Agnes, years later, ministering to the poorest of the poor as Mother Teresa in the streets of Calcutta, India. Yes, Christ equipped her and called her to that work, but her calling was a perfect complement to the natural desire for ministry she developed as a child, watching her mother tend to the welfare of others above her own.

Timothy's own spiritual training began at the feet of his mother Eunice and grandmother Lois (2 Timothy 1:5), which no doubt contributed to the qualifications he had to become the Apostle Paul's protégé. Paul gave Timothy the ultimate spiritual commendation when he wrote, "As a son with his father [Timothy] has served with me in the work of the gospel" (Philippians 2:22).

How would a son serve a father? Probably at his side with humility, respect, obedience, cheerfulness, and perseverance. That's what we would expect to find in a truly humble woman, who serves those in authority whether vocationally, spiritually, in the home, or in church. Humility is marked by being more concerned about others than about oneself.

APPLY Like it or not, every parent is a mentor to his or her children. What specific examples of service to others are you demonstrating to your

Be such a man, and live such a life, that if every man were such as you, and every life a life such as yours, this earth would be God's paradise.

Phillips Brooks

children and to others? If you cannot see specific examples now, what can you change to mentor your children by your own humility?

_____

_____

_____

_____

APPLY What did you learn about the "humanness" of the Christian life from Paul's words in Philippians 2:23 where he wrote, "as soon as I see how things go with me"? If the Apostle Paul didn't always know how things would "go," why should we?

_____

_____

_____

_____

_____

Responding to Scripture

How would you summarize Paul's main theme or idea in Philippians 2:19–24?

_____

_____

_____

_____

_____

Responding to Life

What do you find in this idea that you can apply to your life today or this week?

_____

_____

_____

_____

_____

Responding to God

 Heavenly Father, My desire is for You to view me the same way Paul viewed Timothy, as someone who takes a genuine interest in the welfare of others. I don't desire that for the sake of my pride, but rather because I know it's how Jesus wants to live and bless people through me. Please teach me how to exhibit a humble, servant spirit toward those for whom I have responsibility, especially my family. I ask this for the glory of Christ through me, in his name. Amen.

EPAPHRODITUS (PHILIPPIANS 2:25–30)

Word Study
EPAPHRODITUS

"Epaphroditus" is a Greek name that originally meant "loved by Aphrodite," the Greek goddess of love, beauty, and sexuality. The name itself eventually came to mean "lovely" or "charming." But this pagan name may be an indicator of Epaphroditus' non-spiritual background before meeting Christ.

Put Yourself in Their Shoes
EPAPHRODITUS JOURNEY TO ROME

There is no indication in Philippians that Epaphroditus arrived in Rome with others from Philippi. Indeed, Philippians 4:18 suggests Epaphroditus arrived alone. By sea, the journey from Philippi to Rome would have been well over one thousand miles and taken many days. Compared to the ease of travel today, Epaphroditus' efforts to serve Paul were amazing.

Epaphroditus was a Gentile believer with a humble servant's heart. He may have been the pastor of the Philippian church, or at least one if its leaders. When he heard Paul had been imprisoned in Rome, he made the long journey from Philippi to Rome to carry gifts and supplies to Paul and to encourage him in the Lord. Unfortunately, while Epaphroditus was in Rome, he became seriously ill "and almost died" (Philippians 2:27). According to Paul in that same verse, "God had mercy on him…" and he survived. The Philippian church got word of Epaphroditus' illness and conveyed their concern to him in Rome. That made him all the more eager to return to Philippi to allay their concerns for his health.

When Epaphroditus returned to Philippi, he carried with him the letter we are now studying, which contained this message from Paul about their servant-leader: "Welcome him [Epaphroditus] in the Lord with great joy, and honor men like him, because he almost died for the work of Christ, risking his life to make up for the help you could not give me" (Philippians 2:29–30). Epaphroditus was a man who set aside his own needs and comfort in order to spend weeks with Paul in Rome. His actions were a stellar example of what a humble servant of Christ and others can look like.

SERVICE AND SACRIFICE

But I think it is necessary to send back to you Epaphroditus, my brother, fellow worker and fellow soldier, who is also your messenger, whom you sent to take care of my needs. For he longs for all of you and is distressed because you heard he was ill. Indeed he was ill, and almost died. But God had mercy on him, and not on him only but also on me, to spare me sorrow upon sorrow. (Philippians 2:25–27)

"Brother, fellow worker and fellow soldier." All of these names describe how Paul felt about Epaphroditus. From this choice of words, it is easy to see how much Epaphroditus meant to him. When I think of the lengths Epaphroditus was willing to go to for Paul, the word that comes first to my mind is "sacrifice." I am always amazed when I read stories of people, whether in ancient or present times, who risked their lives for the cause of Christ—those who never looked back when they set out on a mission for God. Even if it turned out that their lives or possessions were spared, the point is they were willing to give up everything. They are not like the man Jesus described in Luke 9:62 who "puts his hand to the plow and looks back." Such a one, Jesus said, is not "fit for service in the kingdom of God." Epaphroditus was not such a person. He was willing to give it all in service to Jesus Christ and His church.

Sadly, in our Western culture, we are rarely called upon to sacrifice for Christ. When we do give of our time, talent, or treasure, it is often out of our abundance and surplus and not out of sacrifice. We have much to learn from saints like Epaphroditus and others in the early church who sacrificed out of their "extreme poverty" (2 Corinthians 8:2).

I read a story about a wealthy man who stood on a wharf watching a huge ship as it left the harbor and headed toward the open sea. A friend of his saw him and asked why he stood at the wharf. The wealthy man replied, "There is $10,000 of medical equipment on that ship I am sending to a hospital in China." There was a moment of silence, after which the other man said, "I, too, am sending a gift to China on that boat. My only daughter is going as a missionary." The wealthy man placed a hand on his friend's shoulder and said, "And I thought *I* had made a sacrifice!"

There are different kinds of sacrifices made for the sake of Christ, all of which are worthy. But the greatest is the one Jesus described in John 15:13: "Greater love has no one than this, that he lay down his life for his friends." That was the kind of friend Epaphroditus was to Paul, one who was prepared to be a living sacrifice for Christ's sake (Romans 12:1).

APPLY What kind of sacrifice(s) have you made for others in the name of Christ? How have others made sacrifices for you?

_____

_____

_____

_____

📖 In what ways besides death might one "lay down his life for his friends" (John 15:13)?

_____

_____

_____

_____

HEALED AND HEADED HOME

Therefore I am all the more eager to send him, so that when you see him again you may be glad and I may have less anxiety. Welcome him in the Lord with great joy, and honor men like him, because he almost died for the work of Christ, risking his life to make up for the help you could not give me. (Philippians 2:28–30)

I have never been to war, nor has my husband. So I have no first-hand experience from which to speak. But from what I have read, war has a bonding effect on those who share its stress and pressure—especially watching a comrade wounded or killed,—like no other experience. It's no surprise that one of the most powerful series of films ever made about war is titled *Band of Brothers*, the mini-series for television that chronicles a company of soldiers during World War II. "Band of brothers" is what we might call Paul and Epaphroditus, or Paul and all those with whom he co-labored in spreading the Gospel.

The Bible pictures the work of spreading the Gospel and living the Christian life as warfare. We develop the deepest ties with those who work with us in that combat. Paul, no doubt, labored intensely in prayer in Rome for his "brother, fellow worker, and fellow soldier" Epaphroditus when he lay ill. Epaphroditus was like a wounded fellow soldier to Paul, and the apostle did everything he could to preserve the life of the one who risked so much, even his own life, to minister to him.

"The sign of our professed love for the gospel is the measure of sacrifice we are prepared to make in order to help its progress."

Ralph Martin

"Self-denial is not so much an impoverishment as a postponement. We make a sacrifice of present good for the sake of a future and greater good."

George Müller

Warfare, whether physical or spiritual, demands a rare kind of humility: the willingness to lay down one's life for country or kingdom or for one's fellow soldiers. That was the humility of Epaphroditus.

📖 Based on Christ's words in Luke 14:31–33, what kind of costs should the Christian count before going into spiritual battle?

_____

_____

_____

_____

List the sacrifices that would be most costly to you if you were called upon to make them for the sake of Christ or others.

_____

_____

_____

_____

Responding to Scripture

How would you summarize Paul's big idea or main theme in Philippians 2:25–30?

_____

_____

_____

_____

_____

Responding to Life

What specific aspect of that theme can you apply to your life immediately or in the days ahead?

_____

_____

_____

_____

_____

Responding to God

 Heavenly Father, I thank You for saints like Epaphroditus and the many others through the centuries who have risked everything and often paid the ultimate price for the sake of Christ and His Gospel. I am in awe of the courage and commitment of those who have been willing to lay down their lives. I pray You will create in me a passion to be a soldier for the Lord, who counts the cost and says, "Yes, I will give it all." Help me not to love this life more than I love you, your Son, the Holy Spirit, and the spreading of Your Word. I pray in Jesus' name. Amen.

REVIEW FOR FOLLOWING GOD

Humility is essential for the follower of Christ. Just as Jesus humbled Himself to the point of death on the cross, we are to pick up our crosses every day by emptying our old selves of our selfish ways and walk in our new resurrected selves and the Christ-centered way. Paul talks about how he humbled himself to have nothing so Christ would be everything. He uses Timothy as an example of a servant leader who also followed in this same path. Epaphroditus, an everyday believer and minister to the Philippian church, was so committed to the cause that he traveled more than a thousand miles alone to minister to Christ's chief apostle in jail. All of these servants thought more about the needs of others than their own needs. Humility is the by-product of following Christ while pride is the by-product of following our own flesh.

Is there an area of your life that is stressful or complicated? If so, pride will insist that you remain in control. Are there things you try to conceal from others? Are there secrets about yourself that you refuse to acknowledge? Hiding our weaknesses only deepens their hold on our lives. Humility brings the strength of God into our lives. It is the cure for the cancer of self-absorption. It opens the way for God's power and grace. The humble have nothing to hide, nor are they ashamed. They know their weaknesses and offer them without reserve to God. God exalts them through their weaknesses by revealing His strength and glory (2 Corinthians 12:7; James 4:6). As long as we refuse to acknowledge our weaknesses, we will never know what it means to experience true joy and freedom in Christ. It's humility that will draw us closer to Christ and show us the way to experience total freedom in this life. [6]

REVIEW OF DAY 1: JESUS (PHILIPPIANS 2:1–11)

Nothing we could suggest or experience on earth could equal the humbling Jesus experienced by leaving the glory of heaven and entering the sin-stained realm called earth. But for purposes of illustration, imagine a couple living in an upscale development with all the finery life has to offer and divesting themselves of most of what they own and moving into the inner city to minister to those without the Gospel. They would trade in a gated, peaceful community for sirens, drugs, sub-standard schools, and people with heartbreaking needs. They would probably feel like Jesus did when He came to earth: "When he saw the crowds, he had compassion on them, because they were harassed and helpless, like sheep without a shepherd" (Matthew 9:36).

There are many Christians who have said "yes" to God when he called them to go into just such an environment—just like Jesus said "yes" when the Father sent him to earth. That's the humility (selflessness) that God honors.

> "A well-grounded assurance of heaven and happiness, instead of puffing a man up with pride, will make and keep him very humble."
>
> **Matthew Henry**

> "It is pride that changed angels into devils; it is humility that makes men as angels."
>
> **St. Augustine**

Put Yourself in Their Shoes

THE CHIEF OF SINNERS

Paul's pride about his achievements as a Pharisee found complete reversal after his encounter with Christ. He wrote to Timothy: "Christ Jesus came into the world to save sinners—of whom I am the worst" (1 Timothy 1:15). Part of humility is being willing to agree with God, no matter how the assessment makes us look or feel. Humility means agreeing with God about the condition that makes us candidates for His grace.

APPLY What is the most humbling thing God has asked you to do for him? How did you respond?

_____

_____

_____

_____

_____

REVIEW OF DAY 2: PAUL (PHILIPPIANS 2:12–18)

There is a danger when reading the Bible's stories to think that the "heroes" of the faith were cut from different cloth than us—that they were stamped from the "hero" mold, and we are stamped from the "plain Christian" mold. That's not true. The Bible makes it clear that God calls and uses ordinary people to accomplish his work.

Paul is a good example of someone who seems beyond normal to us, and that God called him because he was already humble. Yes, he was smart and dedicated and committed—but humble? Not really. Paul describes the prideful life he lived before meeting Christ in Philippians 3:4–6. He also explains that he counted it all as "loss" compared to knowing Christ (Philippians 3:7). So if God can change a prideful person like Paul and use him, God can do the same with us. Paul became humble enough to describe how all his fleshly confidence was insufficient to measure up to God's standards of righteousness (Romans 7).

In Paul's life we can follow the road from pride to humility and see there is hope, by the grace of God, for us.

APPLY Where are you on the road from pride to humility? What "bump" in the road are you currently trying to get over?

_____

_____

_____

_____

_____

REVIEW OF DAY 3: TIMOTHY (PHILIPPIANS 2:19–24)

Anytime I want to encourage my children in the faith, I use the example of Timothy. His humility was not because he was young and intimidated by Paul. Yes, he seems to have had a tendency toward timidity (2 Timothy 1:7). But we have already seen personality traits are not the sign of humility. If anything, Timothy got a good start toward humility through the prayers and training of his mother and grandmother. Indeed, Paul suggests that their influence was a present reality in Timothy's spiritual life (2 Timothy 1:5). Timothy was humble because he had a good foundation in the faith. He knew his place in the order of God's spiritual economy and in his relationship with Paul. He was happy to serve where God had called him.

I have the same desire for my own children—that they would not think of themselves "more highly than … [they] ought, but rather think of …

[themselves] with sober judgment, in accordance with the measure of faith God has given … [them]" (Romans 12:3).

📖 Why is Timothy a good example of the parable Jesus told in Luke 14:7–11? How might you convey the teaching of that parable to your own children?

_____

_____

_____

_____

REVIEW OF DAY 4: EPAPHRODITUS (PHILIPPIANS 2:25–30)

Epaphroditus is an example of a person in Scripture about whom we know very little, yet who had a major impact because of his humble service. (See Romans 16:1–15 for a list of others.)

When I see references to saints in the New Testament who served with little or no recognition, I am reminded of so many women in our Bible study ministry. They serve faithfully behind the scenes or in front of the group, wherever their gifts apply best. Their service is not to promote themselves or the ministry, but to make it possible for an increasing number of women in our community and beyond to come to know Christ in a life-changing way. They, like Epaphroditus, are humble servants of Christ.

📖 How can the words of Jesus in Matthew 6:6 about prayer be expanded to encompass all of our service for him? How are his words motivation for us to serve?

_____

_____

_____

_____

REVIEW PHILIPPIANS 2:1–30

Review the Scriptures and content of this week's lessons and identify three ideas, themes, or action points that struck you from what you studied this week. Especially look for ideas to apply to your own life.

1. _____

_____

_____

_____

_____

2. _____

_____

_____

_____

_____

Did You Know?

? TEACHING CHILDREN

The classic passage on the lifestyle of communicating truth to children is Deuteronomy 6:4–9. There the setting is not a classroom, but the daily activities of a Jewish family in which truth is incorporated in many different ways throughout the day—going out, coming in, lying down, rising up, and everywhere in between. Training children from an early age in truth was a lifestyle, not something on a schedule.

3. _____

_____

_____

_____

_____

REFLECT ON PHILIPPIANS 2:13

For it is God who works in you to will and to act according to his good purpose.

 What do you see God doing in you to accomplish His good purpose in your life?

_____

_____

_____

_____

_____

_____

_____

REMEMBER GOD'S GRACE IN YOUR LIFE

Heavenly Father, I thank You for this week's study on humility. I thank You that humility is not something I have to create in myself, but is something that comes as I learn to submit myself to Your will for my life and become a servant of others for the sake of Christ. I pray for faithful obedience to what You ask me to do, and I pray for a servant's heart to minister wherever and to whomever You direct me—all for the glory of Christ. In his name I pray. Amen.

Philippians 3:1-11

LESSON OVERVIEW

ETERNAL PERSPECTIVE

A pastor once told an older gentleman "Sir, at your age, you need to be thinking about the hereafter." The older gentleman replied, "Oh, pastor, I do all the time! Wherever I go, whatever room I am in—my living room, kitchen, upstairs, or basement—I ask myself, "What am I here after?"

The truth is, many of us believe in a hereafter, but we don't spend a lot of time talking or thinking about it. In this busy, fast-paced life, with all its demands, we rarely are reminded that there is a life after this one unless we're at a funeral, and that *this* life affects *that* one.

Our perspective about eternity is what shapes our priorities in the present. Paul reminds us to live life with eternity in view when he writes, "So we fix our eyes not on what is seen, but on what is unseen. For what is seen is temporary, but what is unseen is eternal" (2 Corinthians 4:18). If we regularly fix our eyes on God and His will for our lives (by listening to Him, remaining obedient to His word, and talking to Him through prayer), we will see each moment as an opportunity to follow Paul's instruction.

Jesus said, "For where your treasure is, there your heart will be also" (Matthew 6:21). If you want a heart for a business, then buy stock in it. If you want a heart for your home, then invest your time and money in it. If you want a heart for God and His kingdom, then put your treasures where God is at work and live with eternity in view.

PROTECTION AGAINST EVIL (PHILIPPIANS 3:1–2)

"Joy is the flag flown from the heart when the king is in residence there."

Principal Rainey

Paul repeats his theme of joy, much like he told the Thessalonians to "Be joyful always" (1 Thessalonians 5:16). Paul reminds us to rejoice, even when times are hard. How do we do that? By remembering where we place our hope.

Watchman Nee, a Chinese minister, was arrested by the Communist Chinese in 1952 for his professed faith in Christ, as well as his leadership among the church. He was judged, condemned, and sentenced to fifteen years in prison. During all that time, only his wife could visit him. In his final letter, on the day of his death, he alluded to his "joy in the Lord" when he said, "In my sickness, I still remain joyful at heart." Why? Because Watchman Nee knew his hope and future were secure in Christ Jesus no matter what happened to him on earth. Today, more than twenty-three hundred churches claim Watchman Nee's ministry as their founder.[7]

BE JOYFUL

Finally, my brothers, rejoice in the Lord! It is no trouble for me to write the same things to you again, and it is a safeguard for you. (Philippians 3:1)

When Paul says "rejoice in the Lord," the key words are *"in the Lord."* For this type of rejoicing is only possible for those who are *"in* Christ" (Romans 8:1). He did not say, "Rejoice in your family, in your riches, or in your circumstances," which are subject to change. He said, "rejoice *in the Lord."* The Lord's love never changes and never ends, and regardless of circumstance, this is something to be celebrated.

A life in Christ is a life of commitment to God through faith in Christ. True faith in Christ is not a life burdened with pleasing God by what we do, but a life of joy and gratitude for what Christ has already done. This life is only possible when Christ Himself, through the Holy Spirit, comes to dwell within the heart of those who believe in who Christ was and is—the son of the Living God. When we live with Christ today, we also live with Him in eternity. What more do we need to be able to rejoice?

Explain why it is possible for a Christian to rejoice even in the most trying or difficult circumstances:

_____

_____

_____

_____

📖 If it seems impossible to rejoice in your present circumstance, according to Psalm 51:12, what else can you do about it?

_____

_____

Beware

Watch out for those dogs, those men who do evil, those mutilators of the flesh.
(Philippians 3:2)

Paul now warns the Philippians to beware of legalizers. He should know; he was one. Beware of those who say it is what you do that gets you into heaven. It is absolutely not. It's what Christ did for us that makes Him the only way to God.

In this verse Paul is expressing his great concern about false teachers. Paul calls the false teachers "dogs, those men who do evil, those mutilators of the flesh" (a reference to circumcision in compliance with Jewish law). Those descriptions seem harsh, especially given how graciously Paul refers to those who stirred up trouble by preaching with impure motives. Do you remember what Paul wrote in Philippians 1:18? "But what does it matter? The important thing is that in every way, whether from false motives or true, Christ is preached." Paul is so gracious in chapter one. Why is he so harsh in chapter three?

The false teachers in chapter three are not preaching Christ alone through faith. They're preaching heresy, a salvation based on works. They are saying what we *do* saves us, and our faith in Jesus Christ is not enough.

Though you may hear the expression, "Just have faith," it's so important to understand that the content of what we believe really does matter. The Bible makes it clear God has been concerned about the true Gospel message from the beginning. In fact, Jesus offers a sobering warning in Matthew 7:

> *Not everyone who says to me, "Lord, Lord," will enter the kingdom of heaven, but only he who does the will of my Father who is in heaven. Many will say to me on that day, "Lord, Lord, did we not prophesy in your name, and in your name drive out demons and perform many miracles?" Then I will tell them plainly, "I never knew you. Away from me, you evildoers!"*
> *(Matthew 7:21–23)*

The one thing that's clear here is that not everyone who claims to know Jesus really does. Some people look like Christ followers, but they're not authentic. One day, Jesus will say, "Away from me; I never knew you." Are your knees shaking? They should be. We need wisdom, and we need to know the truth of God's Word. The Bible says, "Examine yourselves to see whether you are in the faith; test yourselves" (2 Corinthians 13:5). Yes, what we believe makes a difference—that's why Paul gets so worked up. Some think doctrinal error is trivial, but it can, in fact, be a matter of eternal life and death.

Now Paul says he wants to write "the same things" (Philippians 3:1) again. He's referring back to Philippians 1:27–28 when he wrote, "Whatever happens, conduct yourselves in a manner worthy of the gospel of Christ. . . contending as one man for the faith of the gospel without being frightened in any way by those who oppose you." Paul alludes to certain opponents in this passage. But now he brings them back up again as a safeguard so the Philippians don't get sidetracked.

Doctrine
CIRCUMCISION

Circumcision was originally instituted as a sign that a male was part of the community of faith in Israel (Genesis 17:9–14). When Jews began believing in Jesus, some Jews felt the necessity to bring the ordinance of circumcision into the Church for the same purpose: to identify those who were part of the true faith. On many occasions, Paul addressed this issue, saying circumcision was not necessary for Christian men, whether Jew or Gentile (Romans 2:25–29, 4:9–16; Galatians 2:3–5, 5:2–12, 6:12–15). The first Church council in Jerusalem decided that circumcision was not an obligation for Gentile Christians (Acts 15:22–29).

"Do with your hearts as you do with your watches. Wind them up every morning by prayer, and at night examine whether your hearts have gone true all that day."

Thomas Watson

Word Study

DOGS

"Dogs" was a term normally used by Jews to describe Gentiles, denoting the "unclean" status of Gentiles (Mark 7:27–28). But here Paul turns the term back on the Jews themselves. The kind of dogs referred to here were feral animals, traveling in packs and living as scavengers off of what could be found in garbage dumps. False teachers normally travelled in groups as well, picking off unsuspecting believers.

"Compare Scripture with Scripture. False doctrines, like false witnesses, agree not among themselves."

William Gurnall

To make his point, notice the three phrases he uses to describe false teachers (Philippians 3:2):

- The term "dogs" was used for the scavenger dogs that plagued ancient cities. In many small towns in Mexico and South America, wild packs of dogs roam the streets. They're called *perros callejeros* or street dogs. That's the idea behind the word in verse two. These dogs can be vicious and dangerous.

- The second description is "men who do evil." These men were intent on leading people astray from the true Gospel of Christ by faith alone. Notice Paul doesn't call these false teachers misguided or off-base. He calls them evil.

- The third phrase is "mutilators of the flesh." These opponents were a group known as the Judaizers who persistently followed Paul. The Judaizers denied the Gospel of grace. They taught it was necessary to be circumcised and to keep the Law of Moses to be saved. In their minds, Jesus was not sufficient. They taught a person needed Christ plus the Law to be saved. That is not unlike our world today; most cults and other religions are performance-based. But God, from the beginning, has been primarily concerned with our hearts.

Why is it possible to be deceived by false teachers who do not preach the Gospel of grace? (See 2 Corinthians 11:13–15.)

_____

_____

_____

What is your best defense against false teachers? (See Ephesians 6:13–17.)

_____

_____

_____

Responding to Scripture

In your own words, summarize the theme or big idea of Philippians 3:1–2.

_____

_____

_____

_____

Responding to Life

How would your life be different if you applied that theme to your life today?

_____

_____

_____

_____

_____

Heavenly Father, I praise You today that it is possible to rejoice in the Lord Jesus Christ, regardless of my circumstances. I am thankful not to have to depend on things that can change in my life in order to experience Your deep joy and contentment. Because joy is rooted in truth, help me be on guard against any person or teaching that would tempt me to rely on anything except Your grace and my salvation by faith in Christ. Thank You that Jesus has done all the work that is needed for me to be saved. I pray this in His name. Amen.

> **"Legalism is self-righteousness. It is the belief that God is satisfied with our attempt to obey a moral code."**
>
> **Erwin W. Lutzer**

PREVENTING LEGALISM (PHILIPPIANS 3:3–7)

Philippians 3:1–11

DAY TWO

"Legalism will be present wherever a person is trying to be ethical in his own strength, that is without relying on the merciful help of God in Christ. Simply put, moral behavior that is not from faith is legalism. The legalist is always a very moral person. In fact the majority of moral people are legalists because their so called Judeo-Christian morality inherited from their forefathers does not grow out of a humble, contrite reliance on the merciful enabling of God."[7] –John Piper

Perhaps the greatest struggle for the Christian in his every day walk is the tendency toward legalism. We're all wired to be legalists—wired to trust that it's what we do that pleases God. We look to our Bible studies, charitable works, and church attendance as proof of progress in our Christian walk. But though they may create a veneer of Christian substance, these are all about self-reliance. Growing in Christ is about Christ-reliance. Our perpetual tendency seems to be to put confidence in the flesh. But when the Holy Spirit is at work in us, we put our confidence in Jesus. Only He who "began the good work within us" will carry it on to completion as we trust in *Him alone* to do it.

CONFIDENCE IN THE FLESH

> *For it is we who are the circumcision, we who worship by the Spirit of God, who glory in Christ Jesus, and who put no confidence in the flesh—though I myself have reasons for such confidence. If anyone else thinks he has reasons to put confidence in the flesh, I have more: circumcised on the eighth day, of the people of Israel, of the tribe of Benjamin, a Hebrew of Hebrews; in regard to the law, a Pharisee; as for zeal, persecuting the church; as for legalistic righteousness, faultless. (Philippians 3:3–6)*

If anyone understood the legalistic life—putting hope in abilities and achievements—it was Paul. When Paul mentions "flesh," he is referring to his unredeemed humanness and his accomplishments apart from God. Paul gives an outstanding list of credentials and achievements to prove he did everything possible to be righteous. He had the outward sign of circumcision

Did You Know?

? GAMALIEL

In Acts 22:3 Paul says he was "thoroughly trained in the law of our fathers" by Gamaliel, a famous Jewish rabbi. Gamaliel was a Pharisee and respected Jewish teacher, the grandson of Hillel, the most famous Jewish rabbi in Jesus' day. Rabbinic tradition equated Hillel with Moses and Ezra. Gamaliel was one of only seven rabbis to be given the title "Rabban." To be Gamaliel's student made Paul one of the most promising Pharisees in his day.

as a member of the covenant community in accordance with the law. He was a member of the house of Israel, born from the tribe of Benjamin, and was a pure Hebrew (both parents were full-blooded Israelites, committed to religious purity). As a Pharisee, he was a member of the strictest, most orthodox sect in Judaism. And his zeal was proven by his intense persecution of the fledgling Christian church. He had become the most moral and religious person possible.

But after his encounter with Jesus on the road to Damascus, Paul knew he had to "lose his religion." God did not want his sacrifices or his external achievements. God wanted him. He wanted Paul's whole heart. God wanted him to recognize, worship, and love His Son Jesus, who alone made the only sacrifice and achievement that mattered.

Even today, we often focus on our own external accomplishments and abilities to measure our progress in life. We raise, and sometimes push, our children to do well in academics, athletics and appearances. Often their external accomplishments are at the expense of internal regression in character development. We believe we are pleasing God with all our many good deeds, when all God wants is for us to love him so he can do good deeds through us.

On one of D.L. Moody's western evangelistic campaigns, he was followed from city to city by an aged and broken man of venerable appearance who, in each place, asked the privilege of saying a word to the great congregations. The man had a son who had left him years ago. So he would stand up and in a quivering voice say, "Is my son George in this place? O George, are you here? O George, if you are here, come to me. Your old father loves you and can't die content without seeing you again." Then the old man would sit down. One night, a young man came to Mr. Moody's hotel and asked to see him. It was George. When the great evangelist asked him how he could treat a loving father with such cruel neglect, the young man said, "I never thought of him. But, Mr. Moody, I have tried to do all the good I could." That is a picture of a self-righteous prodigal. He was generous with his money and his words, yet every moment of his infamous life, he trampled on the heart of a loving father.[8]

What reasons do you have for putting confidence in your flesh? How can you guard against yielding to that temptation?

_____

_____

_____

_____

CONFIDENCE IN CHRIST

But whatever was to my profit I now consider loss for the sake of Christ. (Philippians 3:7)

Paul makes one thing clear—nothing is more important for the Christian than his faith. Everything Paul thought was important before is nothing compared to knowing Christ and being found in Him. Just as we are saved by faith, we are now called to walk by faith. When Paul was at the end of his life, he said, "I have fought the good fight, I have finished the race, I have

---

Word Study
FLESH

The term "flesh" is used in several ways in the New Testament. Physically, it refers to the human body (Matthew 26:41). Spiritually, it represents human nature absent the Spirit of God and inclined toward sinful disobedience. The works of the flesh (Galatians 5:19–21) are in conflict with (Galatians 5:16–18) the fruit of the Spirit (Galatians 5:22–23).

kept the faith" (2 Timothy 4:7). He did not say, "I established churches, I wrote many epistles, preached many sermons, suffered much persecution." He simply said, "I have kept the faith." That was all that counted toward righteousness in God's sight—faith in Christ alone.

📖 Read 2 Timothy 4:7 and write in your own words what it means to "keep the faith":

_____

_____

_____

We sometimes forget to abide in Christ and consequently believe that we are totally responsible for producing spiritual fruit in our lives. As a Bible teacher, it is easy for me to think that knowledge, experience, and communication skills are what I need to draw others to Jesus. But only when I humble myself and depend totally on God's grace does the Holy Spirit come to enlighten my heart and draw others to Him. Otherwise we would always depend on our flesh.

A person in Christ knows our righteousness is not *before* God as something we present to Him. Our righteousness is *in* God, something God bestows upon us. This makes all the difference in the world. This took Paul the zealot from being a persecutor and murderer of Christians to Paul the apostle, someone full of love, overflowing with compassion and completely dependent on Christ. It also will change a Bible teacher from a proud performer into a humble listener and encourager in the faith.

APPLY What did you once consider "profit" in your life that you now consider "loss for the sake of Christ"?

_____

_____

_____

_____

Responding to Scripture

How would you summarize what Paul is communicating in Philippians 3:3–7?

_____

_____

_____

_____

Responding to Life

How might your life and ministry be different if you applied Paul's words today?

_____

_____

"Just as the sinner's despair of any help from himself is the first prerequisite of a sound conversion, so the loss of all confidence in himself is the first essential in the believer's growth in grace."

A. W. Pink

_____
_____
_____
_____
_____

Responding to God

 Heavenly Father, please show me the areas of my life where I put "confidence in the flesh." I am grateful for the gifts You have given me, but I want to use them to serve You, not to impress You or earn Your favor. I ask You to call to my attention whenever I'm tempted to rely on myself instead of Jesus for my righteous standing in Your sight. Thank You for granting me acceptance by Your grace instead of by my works. In Christ's name I pray. Amen.

Philippians 3:1-11

DAY THREE

THE POWER OF KNOWING CHRIST (PHILIPPIANS 3:8–9)

When the economy struggles, there is no end to the advice about what to do. Should you buy or sell? Should you take risks or sit tight? But Jesus asks a great question: What good is it for you to gain the whole world, yet forfeit your soul? (Mark 8:36). Despite all the advice from economists, what would the Scriptures say? They would say sell, sell, sell and invest in the church. You get a far better rate of return for a far longer period of time in God's economy.

In this passage, Paul is encouraging us to think about our profit and loss accounts. He is saying, "Weigh seriously the values that control your decisions and directions." On Judgment Day, will your credits outweigh your debits? What if they don't? The absolute best investment is the time you spend in pursuit of a close relationship with Jesus Christ. On this, you can never lose.

INTIMACY PRECEDES ACTIVITY

> *What is more, I consider everything a loss compared to the surpassing greatness of knowing Christ Jesus my Lord, for whose sake I have lost all things. I consider them rubbish, that I may gain Christ. (Philippians 3:8)*

Paul acknowledges that all his efforts toward pleasing God have been a waste. When we focus on religious activity for Christ rather than a relationship with him, we fall into legalism. Only in dependence on Him do we gain the very things we were so busy trying to obtain on our own–value, acceptance, and love. Jesus said, "But seek first his kingdom and his righteousness, and all these things will be given to you as well" (Matthew 6:33). Intimacy with Christ leads to righteousness with God; activity without intimacy leads to legalism.

I remember talking with a young wife who had shared some frustrations with her husband. She explained he was so busy she never saw him. Even when he was around, he was mentally somewhere else. In a heated argument they had as a result of her frustration, he finally exclaimed, "I am working hard, I do have to travel, and yes, I even have to be gone on the weekends. But who do you think I am doing all this for?" Her husband's focus was on doing things *for* his wife, yet not spending anytime *with* his wife. When Christians move from legalistic, performance-based dependence on the flesh to a grace-filled, humble, loving dependence on Christ, they discover an increasing desire for intimacy with Him. Only then are they in a right relationship with God.

Once we walk with this desire to know Jesus more and more, the Holy Spirit—the Spirit of Christ—transforms us slowly into His image. This power within helps us to walk by faith and not by sight. It helps us to know Him, not to know about Him.

APPLY What have you lost by becoming a Christian? What "rubbish" can you identify that you gladly have given up?

_____

_____

_____

_____

APPLY How often do you feel you really desire Jesus? How much do you feel you depend on Him?

_____

_____

_____

_____

FAITH BRINGS RIGHTEOUSNESS

> *And be found in him, not having a righteousness of my own that comes from the law, but that which is through faith in Christ—the righteousness that comes from God and is by faith. (Philippians 3:9)*

Our gracious God makes righteousness so simple. We're the ones who make it complicated, and oh how complicated we make it. He simply wants our *faith* in Christ. He says, "For it is by grace you have been saved, through faith—and this not from yourselves, it is the gift of God—" (Ephesians 2:8). But what exactly is righteousness by faith? Dallas Willard in *The Divine Conspiracy* explains this is where the Pharisees and the Scribes missed it. Their fundamental mistake was in focusing on the actions that the law requires and making elaborate specifications of exactly what those actions should be. Then they bound them on others. But, Willard says, "to succeed in keeping the law, one must aim at something other and something more. One must aim to become the kind of person from whom the deeds of the law naturally flow. The apple tree naturally and easily produces apples because of its inner nature. This is the most crucial thing to remember if we would understand Jesus' picture of the kingdom heart...."[9] We seek Jesus and obtain His righteousness. In doing this, we become like Him, and in so

"*Nearness to Christ, intimacy with him, assimilation to his character—these are the elements of a ministry of power.*"
Horatius Bonar

doing, we keep the law, not by trying, but because it is our nature to do so. We trust His promise to make us righteous is enough.

When my nephew, Parker, was leaving for college, he needed a car. The one he had was too old and completely broken down. I had always wanted to surprise him with a special gift because he was such a fine young man, humble and hard-working. So I finally sent him a letter saying we wanted to give him my daughter's car. When he told his parents he had a car, they said, "Where is it?" He said, "I have one because it says so in this letter from Aunt Nancy." Parker understood the same thing that guarantees our righteousness by faith: a promise was made to him, and he believed it.

We, too, have a letter. This letter promises us eternal life if we believe the promise (John 3:16). If you've committed your life to Christ and accepted him as your Savior, you have the gift of eternity. How do you know? Because your letter—the Bible— says so. If you believe it, you have it. You are righteous (right with God) because you trust what He has said.

APPLY Was it easy for you to simply believe in Christ for salvation rather than trying to work for it? Why?

_____

_____

_____

_____

We often quote John 3:16, but if you read the verse that follows, does it have more meaning? How so?

_____

_____

_____

_____

Responding to Scripture

How would you summarize what Paul is saying in Philippians 3:8–9?

_____

_____

_____

_____

_____

Responding to Life

How would your life be different in thought or behavior by applying these verses to your life?

_____

_____

_____

_____

Responding to God

 Heavenly Father, I praise You for putting such an exchange in place—the "rubbish" of my self-righteousness for the righteousness of Christ that comes by faith. I thank You that You don't ask me to work and prove my righteousness to You, because I never could. But you ask me to simply believe in the promise You have made, that if I will believe in Christ, You will count me as righteous in Your sight. That is something I gladly do, in Jesus' name. Amen.

PARTICIPATE IN HIS SUFFERING (PHILIPPIANS 3:10–11)

here is a misconception among new Christians that once you turn your life over to Christ, you will be protected from all harm and pain. If anything, your journey will likely be quite the opposite. As James put it: it's not a matter of *if* you suffer, but *when* (James 1:2). Everything you do now has eternal significance. While you are becoming more and more like Christ, when you walk with Him, there is always a price to pay, because you are walking against what is "normal" in this world. Yet as you grow in this relationship, like Paul you welcome–even desire–whatever it takes to bring you closer to Christ.

SHARING IN HIS SUFFERING

I want to know Christ and the power of his resurrection and the fellowship of sharing in his sufferings, becoming like him in his death. (Philippians 3:10)

First and foremost, Paul wants to know Christ. He does not want to know *about* Him. He wants to know Him personally. He wants to experience Him. He wants to be found *in* Him, to experience that union that is only made possible because God imputed the righteousness of Christ to Paul by faith. Paul wants to know the power of Christ, the same power that raised Jesus from the dead. As growing Christians, we also desire to know Christ and experience His power. But why would anyone want to share in his suffering?

Had Paul not suffered enough? Even after his conversion, Ananias gave him a warning from the Lord about "how much he must suffer for my name" (Acts 9:16). He would endure even more than rejection and shame. He would be shipwrecked, stoned, and beaten, and he would endure affliction in his body and soul. But Paul believed "our present sufferings are not worth comparing with the glory that will be revealed in us" (Romans 8:18). The reward of being in Christ far outweighed the cost of being without Him.

Philippians 3:1–11

Word Study
FELLOWSHIP

Many Christians are familiar with the Greek word for "fellowship," *koinonia*. It comes from another word that refers to a sharer or partner. Therefore, those who fellowship together share in a common experience. In this case, the common experience is suffering. As we share in Christ's suffering, we also share in the power of His resurrection by which suffering is overcome or endured. Fellowship isn't coffee and doughnuts–it's a sharing and joining at the most intimate level possible.

"There is a certain kind of maturity that can be attained only through the discipline of suffering."

D. A. Carson

> **"Without a doubt, what helps us most in accepting and dealing with suffering is an adequate view of God— learning who he is and knowing he is in control."**
>
> **Joni Eareckson Tada**

Doctrine
GOD'S PURPOSE

Romans 8:28 is a favorite verse for Christians as it assures them God will bring good out of the suffering of those called according to His purpose. But too often it is disconnected from the following verse that explains what God's purpose is—"to be conformed to the likeness of His Son" (Romans 8:29). We share in His suffering in order to one day share in his likeness.

"Suffering" here can simply mean preventing ourselves from following sin and self (1 Peter 4:19). That is, we are to identify with Christ by not only verbally assenting to what he did for us on the cross, but also by daily experiencing the crucifying of our "self." In other words, we are to bear our own crosses and follow Jesus (Matthew 16:24).

Suffering can also mean all out torment, whether from illness or persecution or other causes. During these moments, we can feel the presence of Jesus during our lowest times. This brings joy to circumstances in which otherwise, we might never have the ability to find happiness. This is why the Bible says, "Consider it pure joy, my brothers, whenever you face trials of many kinds" (James 1:2). The joy, we discover, is that He has been there all along. He makes himself known, because He knows we can't bear to endure without Him. These precious moments can sustain us for months—even years—until we recognize God's presence again.

Hebrews 5:8 says of Jesus, "Although he was a son, he learned obedience from what he suffered…" Are you willing to learn obedience this way? It could cost a great deal, maybe everything. But through suffering you gain not only abundant life, but the ability to abide in God's presence. Paul could actually rejoice in his suffering because he understood the true meaning and value of suffering. He wrote, "If we died with him, we will also live with him; if we endure, we will also reign with him" (2 Timothy 2:11b–12a).

APPLY What encouragement do you find in the fact that Christ had to learn obedience through suffering?

_____

_____

_____

_____

SHARING IN HIS DEATH

And so, somehow, to attain to the resurrection from the dead. (Philippians 3:11)

When we allow suffering to enter our lives, God is able to conform us to his death. "Conforming us to His death" means personally to walk out Christ's death in our lives. It means dying daily as Paul says in 1 Corinthians 15:31. It means replacing our self-centered ways with Christ-centered ways. As James says, it even means we will *"consider it pure joy . . . whenever . . . [we] face trials of many kinds"* (James 1:2).

Why? We are becoming more and more like him, even unto death. Oswald Chambers wrote, "A saint's life is in the hands of God like a bow and arrow of an archer. God is aiming at something the saint cannot see and he stretches and strains the saint. Often the saint thinks he cannot take anymore. Then God continues to stretch until his purpose is in sight, and then he lets us fly."[10]

Once you have felt His presence in your pain, you realize there was a purpose. No matter how small or large, no matter how you feel, God is working out everything that happens for your good (Romans 8:28). He is "conforming you unto his death." This is how God works. He creates life out of death. He creates beauty out of ashes.

Jesus said, "I tell you the truth, unless a kernel of wheat falls to the ground and dies, it remains only a single seed. But if it dies, it produces many seeds" (John 12:24.) God will bring you through seasons where it looks like all has been lost and everything looks hopeless. Yet, there will come a time when God will "resurrect" an area of your life. That portion of your life will grow; you will treat it differently. You will use it to help others, and it will multiply.

When you and I believed in Christ, we died with Him on the cross. We were then raised with Him as we began our new life. When we walk with Christ, we carry our crosses and die daily to self.

I've often derived comfort from one of the most painful scenes in the Bible—the Garden of Gethsemene. The fact that Jesus cried out to God and prayed, "[N]ot my will, but yours be done" (Luke 22:42) gives me freedom to approach God honestly as many times as I need.

As a mother and grandmother of several precious children, I have been on my knees before God on behalf of my children, calling out for Him to guide and direct them on their journeys, to protect them, and deliver them from adversity. Yet each time that I slowly die to my own will and surrender to God's, I experience what Paul meant about "being conformed to his death." I die to what I want in exchange for what God wants. I die to my expectations and surrender to His plan. I let go of my control and yield to His. I die to self and live in Christ. Through this ongoing process, there is an inner joy and peace that comes from surrender. I begin to see how God's plan is always better than mine. I see Him working things out for good as He promised. We, like Paul, want to know Christ. But in order to have more of Him, there needs to be less of self. As John the Baptist so aptly put it, "He must become greater; I must become less" (John 3:30).

Though dying to self is never easy, let's keep an eternal perspective and always remember the promise Paul made to the Corinthians: "Therefore we do not lose heart. Though outwardly we are wasting away, yet inwardly we are being renewed day by day. For our light and momentary troubles are achieving for us an eternal glory that far outweighs them all. So we fix our eyes not on what is seen, but on what is unseen. For what is seen is temporary, but what is unseen is eternal" (2 Corinthians 4:16–18).

APPLY What did Jesus mean by his illustration of the grain of wheat that dies? How is your life like that grain of wheat?

_____

_____

_____

📖 Put 2 Corinthians 4:16–18 in your own words:

_____

_____

Responding to Scripture

How would you express the heart of Paul's message in Philippians 3:10-11?

_____

_____

Put Yourself in Their Shoes
GOD'S WILL

It is not always God's will to relieve us of the pain of suffering. He didn't spare Christ from pain, nor did he spare the apostle Paul. Paul asked God three times to spare him from a painful situation in his life. Instead of taking away the pain, God gave Paul grace to endure it. And Paul rejoiced, knowing that grace would reveal more of Christ through him than comfort would (2 Corinthians 12:7–10).

"We ought to give ourselves up to God, both in temporal and spiritual things, and seek our satisfaction only in fulfilling His will. Whether He leads us by suffering or consolation, all is the same to one truly resigned."

Brother Lawrence

_____

_____

_____

_____

Responding to Life

What is the best way for you to apply this message to your own life today?

_____

_____

_____

_____

_____

Responding to God

 Heavenly Father, I praise You that it is possible to know Jesus Christ in the most intimate way possible—in the power of His resurrection and the fellowship of sharing in His sufferings. As You gave Jesus power to endure suffering, I pray for power to endure mine. I count it a privilege to become like Christ in His life, His suffering, His death, and His resurrection so the world might witness Your power in and through me for His glory. In Jesus' name I pray. Amen.

Philippians 3:1-11

DAY FIVE

"Every action of our lives touches on some chord that will vibrate in eternity."

E. H. Chapin

REVIEW FOR FOLLOWING GOD

Jim Elliot, a missionary whose story is best known from the 2006 movie *End of the Spear*, focused his life on eternity. After changing his major in college to better help him follow Christ and serve as a missionary, he spent time studying Greek in order to better understand deeper things in the Bible. He also added language acquisition to help him reach people with whom he did not share a common language. His heart became fixed on reaching the Waodani Indians of Ecuador, a tribe known for violence and its hatred of outsiders. He said of the risk he was taking, "I seek not a long life, but a full life, like that of Jesus Christ." Elliot was killed by the Waodani in 1956 just months after he began to reach out and interact with the tribe.

Someone who lives with an eternal perspective is more concerned with the things of God's kingdom than being too dedicated to things on this earth. Though it may sound crass, it is true that Elliot got what he sought—a short life full of dedication to the one who had saved his life. Eventually, many of those Indians came to know Christ, and Elliot's life has inspired generations to live with eternity in view. His short life strongly resembles the short life of our Lord and Savior.

There are people in this world who live that way. A mother's car breaks down and she ends up leading the auto mechanic to Jesus. A man, by his godly example in the office, leads an angry boss to the love of Christ. Every moment brings with it an opportunity to spread God's kingdom on this earth. We are called by God to live with eternity in view.

Paul certainly did. Even from prison he spread the Gospel and drew others to Jesus through his letters. He rejoiced in the midst of his difficult circumstances, because his eyes were on the prize set heavenward in Christ Jesus. In this week's lesson, let's look at four strategies that helped Paul keep his focus on eternity.

REVIEW OF DAY 1: PROTECT AGAINST EVIL (PHILIPPIANS 3:1–2)

Paul sought protection. He asked the Philippians for prayer, because he knew he could accomplish nothing on his own. The same is true for us. It's so easy to charge out into the world each day, forgetting our need for protection and guidance. Each day we run into unexpected challenges–gossip, angry drivers, inappropriate media content, constant demands, stressful decisions–all of which throw us into worry and panic. But before we begin the day, before we begin the project, or before we begin research for a cure for a sick friend, there is no better solution or guarantee for success than going before God in prayer. The greatest gift we can give our husbands or children or friends is to lift them up daily in prayer for God's protection. It's also the greatest gift we can give ourselves.

APPLY What is the greatest protection you need from God? How often do you ask him for that protection?

_____

_____

_____

_____

REVIEW OF DAY 2: PREVENT LEGALISM (PHILIPPIANS 3:3–7)

Paul learned not to depend on himself but only on Christ. This is the key to the Christian life—not walking in our own strength, but in the supernatural power of the Holy Spirit. Those who walk in the Spirit will show forth Christlikeness whether they are aware of it or not. This comes about by consciously choosing by faith to rely on the Holy Spirit to guide your every step. Failure to rely on the Holy Spirit results in walking in the flesh, which is legalism or relying on self.

When we do not choose to walk in the Spirit, we grieve the Spirit (Ephesians 4:30), though restoration is available through confession. To prevent this, we walk with the Spirit, allowing Him to guide our steps and conform our mind to godliness as we read God's Word. To walk in the flesh is bondage, but to walk in the Spirit is true freedom. Just as we have received Christ by faith, He asks us to walk by faith with Him each day until we see him face-to-face.

But how do we do this? What does it mean to walk in the Spirit? How does the Holy Spirit guide our steps? The answer is simple yet difficult: we must take time to be still and listen to what he wants to tell us. We must close our mouths, open our Bibles, and wait. This is not a complicated or mysterious task, but it will require a level of discipline that few of us have cultivated.

"Live near to God and all things will appear little to you in comparison with eternal realities."

Robert Murray M'Cheyne

 **Doctrine**
LEGALISM

Jesus' most thorough attack on the legalism of the Pharisees is recorded in Matthew 23 where he recites "seven woes" against the Jewish leaders. These echo six woes voiced by Isaiah against Israel in the Old Testament (Isaiah 5:8, 11, 18, 20, 21, 22). Jesus spared no words, calling the Pharisees hypocrites, blind guides, blind fools, whitewashed tombs, snakes, and vipers.

For those who do cultivate this discipline, however, there are unimaginable rewards.

APPLY When are you most tempted to walk in the flesh–to live in dependence on your own strength instead of Christ?

_____

_____

_____

_____

REVIEW OF DAY 3: POWER OF KNOWING CHRIST (PHILIPPIANS 3:8–9)

Paul's primary goal was to know Jesus better. It's amazing how much time we devote to better know a friend, relative, or someone we admire. But we fall short in getting to know Jesus, the one who loves us more than anyone and who has given us more than anyone. It's not intentional. Deep down, we really would like to know Him. But we let the daily distractions of life steal time away from us. We forget the devil comes to kill, steal, and destroy. So we must discipline ourselves to hear from God and His Word regularly in order to draw closer to our Savior and avoid the temptations of this world.

The more we listen to God, the more we understand, and the more we experience His love and presence. The benefits that come from time spent with Him are immeasurable. We not only become more like Him and experience His power, but we experience a little bit of heaven on earth. One day, when we arrive at heaven's pearly gates, we will see Christ face-to-face and enter the joy of His presence. So why not get an early start on that blessed experience and taste the kingdom right now by getting to know Him while we can?

APPLY Which do you spend the most time doing–getting to know *about* Christ or getting to know Christ? How do you know the difference?

_____

_____

_____

_____

REVIEW OF DAY 4: PARTICIPATE IN HIS SUFFERING (PHILIPPIANS 3:10–11)

Paul wanted to become like Christ—not only in his boldness in ministry but in his courage to accept the cost. Paul said, "To live is Christ, and to die is gain" (Philippians 1:21). How can that be? How can dying be a gain? Because nothing in life was more important to Paul than Christ. Christ and His glory alone were important. Christ was all. You may lose everything in this life, but if all that matters to you is Christ, you have lost nothing. That is why Paul could say, "I consider that our present sufferings are not worth comparing with the glory that will be revealed in us" (Romans 8:18). The love of the Lord is better than life itself (Psalm 63:3).

Jesus said, "Whoever would be my disciple must deny himself—and pick up his cross" (Mathew 16:24). In this life we must be prepared to suffer, be rejected, disciplined, stretched, and to go through many tribulations as we follow Christ. Whether or not it feels like it while we are enduring, we are

Put Yourself in Their Shoes
RESURRECTION

In Philippians 3:11 Paul expresses a hope to "somehow . . . attain to the resurrection from the dead." The use of the word "somehow" is not a statement of uncertainty on Paul's part, as if suffering for Christ was a prerequisite for participating in the resurrection. Rather, it was a reflection of the mystery of fellowship with Christ. We share in His suffering and share in His resurrection. No one was more confident of the resurrection from the dead than Paul (1 Corinthians 15:12–58).

promised our suffering is all worth it. Why? For by his stripes we've been healed (Isaiah 53:5). Our lives have been paid for and at the highest price. We gladly pay through our sufferings out of overwhelming gratitude for what He did, because we know our light and momentary afflictions are nothing in comparison to the eternal weight of glory being produced in us (2 Corinthians 4:17).

APPLY The time to decide on your willingness to suffer for Christ is before the suffering arrives. What price(s) have you paid for identifying with Christ?

_____

_____

_____

_____

What do you think eternal weight of glory might mean? Read 2 Corinthians 4:17 and ask God to reveal some of the changes he works in you when you suffer.

_____

_____

_____

_____

REVIEW PHILIPPIANS 3:1–11

Review the scriptures and content of this week's lessons and identify three ideas, themes, or action points that struck you from what you studied this week. Especially look for ideas to apply to your own life.

1. _____

_____

_____

_____

2. _____

_____

_____

_____

3. _____

_____

_____

_____

_____

> "Heaven will pay for any loss we may suffer to gain it; but nothing can pay for the loss of heaven."
>
> Richard Baxter

Reflect on Philippians 3:8

What is more, I consider everything a loss compared to the surpassing greatness of knowing Christ Jesus my Lord, for whose sake I have lost all things. I consider them rubbish, that I may gain Christ.

 Compare what you have lost with what you have gained as a result of identifying with Jesus Christ. Which is greater?

_____

_____

_____

_____

_____

REMEMBER GOD'S GRACE IN YOUR LIFE

Heavenly Father, I thank You for Your work in changing my perspective from a temporal, earthly one to an eternal, heavenly one. Thank You that this earth is not my home and that I have a heavenly destination, a new life, and a new hope of eternal righteousness in Your presence. Thank You for sending Jesus Christ to take my sin upon Himself so I might take His righteousness as my own. Thank You for giving me the grace to leave earthly things behind and focus on Your heavenly kingdom. In Jesus name I pray. Amen.

Philippians 3:12—4:1

LESSON OVERVIEW
ENDURANCE

Cliff Young grew up poor in the Australian Outback. His family owned a lot of land and sheep, but no horses or tractors. They rounded up their two thousand sheep on foot.

Cliff would often run after those animals for two or three days. He even developed a particular way of running, a kind of shuffle, which helped him conserve energy when he was roaming the countryside for a long time. He knew he wasn't faster than the sheep, so his only hope was to outlast them.

When Cliff was 61 years old, someone told him about a race from Sydney to Melbourne—nearly 550 miles. Elite athletes from all over the world, most of them with major sponsorships, train for years to compete in the five-day event.

Cliff decided to enter. Race officials, other athletes, and the media were initially curious about the old farmer who showed up in overalls and work boots. Imagine their shock as Cliff, with his characteristic shuffle, not only completed the course but won the race in record time. Years of chasing sheep for days at a time had made him able to run while the other athletes slept.

He didn't know there was a $10,000 prize. He gave his winnings away to other runners and endeared himself to his nation. Since that race, many ultra-marathoners have adopted the "Young Shuffle," not knowing it was originally used to help catch sheep.

The kind of endurance that wins races doesn't come without struggle. It was the long, hard days over years of rounding up sheep that made Cliff Young the winner of the Westfield UltraMarathon, and it is years of persisting in our faith during trials that will produce perseverance in us. That perseverance forms our character and gives us hope. Paul makes it clear that we will all suffer for our faith. But Christ's hope, which comes in the midst of our struggles, does not disappoint.

PRESSING ON TOWARD THE HEAVENLY GOAL (PHILIPPIANS 3:12–13)

Dr. Horatius Bonar said he could tell when a Christian was growing. In proportion to the Christian's growth in grace, he would elevate his Master, talk less of what he did or was doing, and become smaller and smaller in his own esteem, until "like the morning star, he faded away before the rising sun."

In the fourth century B.C. a promising Greek artist named Timanthes was under the instruction of a well-known tutor. After many years of study, the young painter created a wonderful portrait he gazed at for days with pride. One morning, to his horror, he discovered the instructor had intentionally ruined his work. With anger and tears, Timanthes demanded the instructor explain his actions. The instructor said the painting was retarding Timanthes' progress. It was excellent but not perfect, so he wanted him to start again. The student did as he was asked and produced what many consider one of the finest paintings of antiquity, "The Sacrifice of Iphigenia." [11]

God's goal for us is nothing less than becoming like Jesus Christ (Romans 8:29). Even though Paul was a godly man and accomplished much, he admitted he needed to advance in holiness. Like Paul, we should not be satisfied with our spiritual attainments, but keep pressing on to become more and more like Christ.

NOTHING ON MY OWN

Not that I have already obtained all this, or have already been made perfect, but I press on to take hold of that for which Christ Jesus took hold of me. (Philippians 3:12)

We cannot make any real progress in the Christian life without total dependence on Christ. Jesus said, ". . . apart from me you can do nothing" (John 15: 5), and that is what Paul was saying here. He could do nothing of any worth without Jesus Christ.

When nineteenth-century evangelist J. Wilbur Chapman was in London, he had an opportunity to meet General William Booth, founder of the Salvation Army, who at that time was eighty years old. Chapman asked the general if he would disclose the secret of his success. "He hesitated a second," Dr. Chapman said, "and I saw the tears roll down his cheeks as he said, 'I will tell you the secret: God has had all there was of me. There have been men with greater brains, men with greater opportunities. But from the day I got the poor of London on my heart, and a vision of what Jesus Christ could do with the poor of London, I made up my mind that God would have all of William Booth there was.' " Dr. Chapman said he went away from that meeting realizing the greatness of a man's power is the measure of his surrender. [12]

When a man is humble and surrendered to God, there is no limit to how God can use him. God said He resists the proud "but gives grace to the humble" (James 4:6). Humility is simply a deep view of our utter unworthiness, an absolute abandonment to God that, without the slightest doubt, He will do the greatest things in us.

Like Paul did in his pre-conversion life, the great reformer Martin Luther tried everything he could to be perfect before God. He fasted, prayed, and denied his self sleep. Like Paul he said, "If anyone could have *earned* heaven as a monk, it was I." But when Martin Luther came across the words in Romans 1:17, "The righteous will live by faith," he realized salvation no longer came by self-effort or sacraments, but by the gift of faith. Humility was no longer a virtue that earned grace but a necessary response to the gift of grace. In this subtle but most important distinction, Luther discovered growth in the Christian life. Just as we live by faith, we now walk by faith (2 Corinthians 5:7). So the only way anyone can make progress in the Christian life is by believing what Paul said was true: *"he who began a good work in you will carry it on to completion until the day of Christ Jesus"* (Philippians 1:6).

Word Study
PRESSING ON

When Paul says he presses on in Philippians 3:12 he uses a Greek word (*dioko*) that can also be translated as "to chase after, to pursue in order to persecute" as it is used in Matthew 23:34. Paul changed from being a pursuer of Christians (Acts 22:4) to a pursuer of Christ to gain whatever Christ had in store for him in his life.

APPLY How would you define "pressing on to take hold of Christ" in your own life? What does "pressing on" look like for you?

_____

_____

_____

_____

_____

APPLY How would you describe a friend who lived his or her life by faith? What does that mean in practical terms?

_____

_____

_____

_____

"Trust the past to the mercy of God, the present to his love and the future to his providence."

St. Augustine

RUNNING THE RACE

> *Brothers, I do not consider myself yet to have taken hold of it. But one thing I do: Forgetting what is behind and straining toward what is ahead. (Philippians 3:13)*

Throughout Scripture, Paul often compares the Christian to a runner whose finish line is heaven (1 Corinthians 9:25–27; Hebrews 12:1–3; 2 Timothy 2:5). Warren Wiersbe says, "Each Christian has a place on the racetrack where they are called to use their gifts of service. Each one has a goal established by Christ. Our task in life is to 'lay hold of that for which Christ laid hold of us'—we begin by forgetting the past—past sins and failures as well as past successes. We must press on in His power." [13]

Recently, I ran my own race. I wanted to get in shape, so I decided to run a half-marathon. After announcing my lofty goal to my family, my four children chimed in one-by-one, saying they wanted to join me. I began to train every day drenched in sweat, exhausted, sore muscles, climbing hills out-of-breath, and slowly the pounds came off. Some days I did not train well at all. But I had to forget the past and keep my focus on what lay ahead. The day of the race finally came. Off we went, squeezing through the crowds, up and down hills, and by the halfway mark, all the kids had passed me. But I kept my eyes on the finish line and crossed it. It was painful, but never had pain felt so good to me.

The Christian life is much like that race and the races Paul refers to. Showing up at the race as a runner is the same as inviting Christ into my life and admitting I am a sinner. Salvation is a one-time event. It's the start of the race. But sanctification is a process, in which our aim is to press on to be like Christ and cross the finish line in His image. The process is not easy. It requires discipline and determination; but the finish is worth the pain, and the goal is worth the aim.

> **APPLY** Have you entered the race through faith in Christ? Are you ahead of the pack, holding your own, or falling behind?

_____

_____

_____

> **APPLY** How would you describe your training regimen for the spiritual race? What spiritual disciplines do you practice regularly to keep yourself in shape?

_____

_____

_____

_____

Responding to Scripture

In your own words, describe the big idea of Philippians 3:12–13?

_____

_____

_____

_____

Responding to Life

How would your life look different if you practiced what Paul writes about in these two verses?

_____

_____

_____

_____

"Christianity is the total commitment of all I know of me to all I know of Jesus Christ."

William Temple

"A conviction is not truly a conviction unless it includes a commitment to live by what we claim to believe."

Jerry Bridges

Heavenly Father, thank You for *desiring* perfection *for* me but not *demanding* perfection *of* me. Thank You for seeing me as one day being like Your Son, Jesus Christ. Thank You for forgiving me when I fail to achieve all You desire for me. Help me, Father, to stay in the race. Grant me the discipline and the determination not to falter, not to look behind, but to stay focused on what lies ahead. I look forward to crossing the finish line by Your grace. In Christ's name I pray. Amen.

PRIZE OF PERSISTENCE (PHILIPPIANS 3:14–15)

When my children were in high school, they would sometimes grow weary in their studies. Even though they knew the goal of completion was a great one, sometimes they would tire out. So I would work to find ways to keep them motivated. I would make them snacks, take them outside for a break, or even take them on a family vacation once exams were over.

Likewise, believers can grow weary in living for Christ. We can wonder why we keep going, why we keep pushing ourselves. But Paul gives us an incentive that will last a lifetime: to press on to win the prize of one day seeing Christ face-to-face and sharing in His eternal glory. If we are able to understand the value of that prize and keep it in mind, we will never have trouble pressing on.

PRESSING FOR THE PRIZE (PHILIPPIANS 3:14)

I press on toward the goal to win the prize for which God has called me heavenward in Christ Jesus. (Philippians 3:14)

Some of us are goal-oriented. We like striving toward a goal and the feeling of accomplishment that comes with each challenging step. The Apostle Paul was like this too. First-century Christians had no problem identifying the passion of his life. His actions matched his goal of winning the prize for which God called him heavenward in Christ Jesus.

Paul was determined to rely on the Holy Spirit's power to get him to his goal, one step at a time, one struggle at a time. None of us has achieved the goal of complete sanctification (Christlikeness). Every step forward is the result of the Holy Spirit at work within us (Galatians 5:22–23). Paul pressed on with determination to reach this goal of ultimate conformity by trusting God to do it as he kept his focus on Christ and His glory. He refused to be inflated by his past achievements as a Pharisee or paralyzed by the guilt of his persecution of Christians. He had "[thrown] off everything that hinders and the sin that so easily entangles . . ." and decided to "run with perseverance the race marked out for us," fixing his "eyes on Jesus, the author and perfecter of our faith" (Hebrews 12:1–2).

Philippians 3:12—4:1

DAY TWO

Doctrine
CHRIST-LIKENESS

The Bible mentions two ways of becoming more like Christ. First, Christ himself lives in Christians: "...I no longer live, but Christ lives in me" (Galatians 2:20). Second, the indwelling presence of the Holy Spirit who manifests the life of Christ through us: "But the fruit of the Spirit is love, joy, peace, patience, kindness, goodness, faithfulness, gentleness and self-control." These nine traits are examples of the character of Christ and are not a conclusive list. There are other "fruits" of the Holy Spirit besides these nine.

Doctrine
FIGHTING THE GOOD FIGHT

To get an idea of the kind of "fight" Paul was involved in, and through which he remained faithful, read these two passages:

• 2 Corinthians 6:3–10
• 2 Corinthians 11:16–33

In 2 Corinthians, Paul is forced to defend his apostleship and cites what he has endured as evidence of one who is committed to running the race until the finish.

As Paul drew closer to the finish line at the end of his life, he admitted the race had not been easy. But he could proclaim, "I have fought the good fight, I have finished the race, I have kept the faith" (2 Timothy 4:7).

APPLY What have you had to "throw off" in your own life that has easily entangled your progress?

_____

_____

_____

The Christian who desires to be like Christ needs only to be faithful in the *process* and trust God for the *product*. It reminds me of these words spelled out in lights at the eighteenth Olympic game in Tokyo in 1964: "The most important thing in the Olympic games is not to win but to take part." Just as the most important thing in life is not the triumph but the struggle. The essential thing is to have "fought well."

As Christians who desire to grow, let's remember our job is to press on. God's job is to conform us *to* Christ as he calls us heavenward *in* Christ.

APPLY Are you goal-oriented by nature? If so, how do you keep the goal described in verse 14 at the top of your list? If not, how do you motivate yourself to pursue that goal?

_____

_____

_____

_____

What had Paul done in the past that might make it hard for him to preach Christ to people? How could that hinder him?

_____

_____

_____

PROCESS OF MATURITY

> *All of us who are mature should take such a view of things. And if on some point you think differently, that too God will make clear to you. (Philippians 3:15)*

Paul exhorted the Philippian believers to take on the same goal as he—to press on toward conformity to Christ. He trusted God to make things clear to those who disagreed with him.

When Paul wrote about maturity, he explained to the Corinthians there are immature Christians and mature Christians (1 Corinthians 3:1–3).

The young Christian is focused on himself, living a life of "mine" in every way, much like a toddler. They often don't listen to their parent(s), so they have little knowledge of God's Word. But the mature believer has his eyes on Jesus, not himself. He listens to Christ daily. His only desire is to please and serve his Lord.

"In my own personal and pastoral experience, I can say I have never known a man or woman who came to spiritual maturity except through discipline."

Donald S. Whitney

Paul told the Corinthians they needed to learn how to take the milk—the basic truths of the Gospel—and practice them. The good news is that our heavenly Father will guide us every step of the way in this process. But God's sovereignty in sanctification does not remove our responsibility. Rather, it enables us: "for it is God who works in you to will and to act according to his good purpose" (Philippians 2:13).

Our level of maturity often depends on our faithfulness to be obedient to God's Word. If we do not act upon what we know to be true to God's Word, we will not grow in the likeness of Jesus Christ. It's simple really. If we love Him, we will obey Him. If we obey Him, we will become like Him.

In spite of all his achievements, Paul acknowledged to the Philippians that all is a loss compared to the greatness of knowing Christ. All is a distraction compared to the single focus of Christ. All of us only grow when we persist in conformity and obedience to Christ.

📖 Based on Paul's words in Philippians 3:15, would you call yourself "mature?" That is, to what degree are you practicing what he wrote in Philippians 3:12–14?

_____

_____

_____

_____

Why does it take a long-term view of life to be a mature Christian? When do you get the "prize"?

_____

_____

_____

Responding to Scripture

How would you describe Paul's main theme or focus in Philippians 3:14–15?

_____

_____

_____

Responding to Life

To what degree is that theme a priority in your life? What do you need to do to make sure it remains a priority?

_____

_____

_____

_____

Put Yourself in Their Shoes

THE PRIZE

In Greek athletic games (the forerunner of the modern Olympics), athletes competed for a crown of leaves or a cash award—something that had short-term value. The prize Paul talks about is heaven: eternal life in the presence of God. In Romans 8:30 Paul refers to this status as being "glorified."

"Many spiritual experiences are possible which do not in and of themselves produce maturity. Rather, it is our response to experience which will determine our progress in maturity."

Sinclair Ferguson

Dear heavenly Father, I thank You for calling me into a relationship with Jesus Christ. I also thank You for calling me to be conformed to the image of Christ for all eternity. I pray for whatever grace is needed for me to understand and embrace the words of Paul in these verses. I want to press on toward the goal. I don't want to fail to finish the race faithfully. Please make clear to me anything I am doing that is impeding Your work in my life. In Jesus' name I pray. Amen.

Philippians 3:12—4:1

DAY THREE

PERCEPTION OF ETERNAL LIVING (PHILIPPIANS 3:16–20A)

Proverbs 23:7 (KJV) says, "As he thinketh in his heart, so is he." The mind is powerful. We are who we think we are. If we carry around baggage and misconceptions about ourselves in our minds, this will surface in how we live. If we want to know what someone believes, we only need look at how they live their life. Their actions will reflect whether they feel loved, accepted, and have a purpose, or whether they are insecure, compulsive, driven, or lacking direction. We all live what we believe.

LIVE WHAT YOU BELIEVE

Only let us live up to what we have already attained. Join with others in following my example, brothers, and take note of those who live according to the pattern we gave you. (Philippians 3:16–17)

Another way Paul could have put this is, "Are you living up to what has already been attained *for* you?" The word "attained" here means "to accomplish something" or "to achieve a goal." Jesus attained salvation for us at the cross. Through His suffering, he made possible our restored relationship with God. He gave us victory, hope, freedom, and joy. But are we living as victors? Do we live with freedom and joy? If we really *believed* what Christ did for us, our lives would reflect it. More often we live as though we're defeated in life—anxious, worried, and stressed. Paul reminds us, "No, in all these things we are more than conquerors through him who loved us" (Romans 8:37).

When we find ourselves living defeated lives, thinking anxious thoughts, or feeling hopeless, our responsibility as believers is to trust God's Word first and to change our thinking about our situations, to take our thoughts captive (2 Corinthians 10:5) and make them obedient to Christ. Our minds can be powerful tools for God, and when we use them to change our thinking, God can change our lives by His truth. As we change our thinking, we begin to live out the truth we now believe, and God's reality comes alive in our lives. This is essential to the believer who takes the Great Commission seriously. If our example is a life of someone stressed out and exhausted, our life is not an example of Christ. If our life is an example of someone who overcomes, that is compelling and may be a witness to lead others to Him.

> **"You can't change the past, but you can ruin a perfectly good present by worrying about the future."**
>
> **Anonymous**

Our perceptions can often be products of how we were raised. I grew up as the oldest child. In that position, I felt the need to please my parents. I tried to be the best at everything. I put pressure on myself to succeed and believed good performance brought love and acceptance. How many children grow up without the unconditional love of a parent? But parents are, after all, only human and usually raise their children the way they were raised. On top of that, children may listen to peers who tell them they are losers or outcasts. These seeds are planted early in their minds, often with negative effects that can last a lifetime.

Therefore, the discovery that we are loved and accepted just as we are by our Heavenly Father can be life-changing and mind-altering.

Oh, the freedom! To learn that He loved us so much that "while we were still sinners" He gave His Son to die for us (Romans 5:8). He loves us not because of who we are but because of who He is. Real love (God's kind of love) comes prior to and apart from anything we do. He is able to do this, because He is love (1 John 4:8, 16).

But even as we grow as Christians in this love, it's easy to forget who we *really* are in Christ. We live in a world that is always telling us differently. Paul wrote, "Those who live according to the sinful nature have their minds set on what that nature desires; but those who live in accordance with the Spirit have their minds set on what the Spirit desires" (Romans 8:5). Our focus affects our behavior. Helen Keller said, "Keep your face to the sunshine and you cannot see the shadows."

Who we listen to the most affects why we think the way we do. Who we hang out with the most affects why we live the way we do. When Paul says, *"Take note of those who live according to the pattern we gave you"*(Philippians 3:17), he is telling us to follow the example of those who live for Christ, and then we will live for him too. As Proverbs 13:20 says, *"He who walks with the wise grows wise, but a companion of fools suffers harm."*

But just as children are easily influenced by their friends, so are immature Christians. Even mature Christians can struggle with this. I knew of a neighborhood where within a distance of just two blocks there were four divorces over a one-year period. All of these couples were friends of each other, had taken vacations together, and gone out to dinners together. Over time, they had picked up one another's values (or lack of values), including infidelity in marriage, and none of their marriages survived the consequences of this kind of thinking.

Paul reminds us to seek good role models, worthy mentors, and quality friends. Look for others who desire to live a life pleasing to Christ, and you will be more likely to do the same.

📖 Read Proverbs 13:20 and write what this might mean for you and your children.

_____

_____

_____

_____

Put Yourself in Their Shoes
INFLUENCE

Paul was not shy about encouraging Christians to follow his example because he followed the example of Christ. Christ is the model (1 Peter 2:21), but we need the example of people like the apostles to serve as examples of Christlikeness (1 Corinthians 11:1; 2 Thessalonians 3:7). The model for discipleship is for new Christians to look to the example of older Christians so that they (the younger) will become older models one day themselves (2 Timothy 2:1–2).

APPLY Which people in your life provide spiritual patterns for you to follow? Who are you influencing positively or negatively by the spiritual life you lead?

_____

_____

_____

_____

LIVE LIKE YOU'RE DYING

For, as I have often told you before and now say again even with tears, many live as enemies of the cross of Christ. Their destiny is destruction, their god is their stomach, and their glory is in their shame. Their mind is on earthly things. But our citizenship is in heaven. (Philippians 3:18–20a)

Paul is sharing his disappointment in the worldly Christian who seeks only to please self. The true Christian lives to please God. One day we will be accountable for the way we lived our lives.

As we get older, it's natural to think more about heaven. After all, we're getting closer to it. My pastor once said you often find senior citizens taking Bible study seriously because they are getting ready for the Big Exam. But Christ came that we may live an abundant life now, not later (John 10:10). The life best lived is the life lived in the moment. This life is heavenly minded and lives each day with eternity in view.

I don't want to live one day that is not pleasing to God, even though I am painfully aware of my daily shortcomings. My thoughts are not always pure. I let the world and others influence me. Power, praise, prominence, and pride sneak their way in, and I begin to covet what the world offers.

But if each day I choose Christ and the power of his Holy Spirit in my life; if each day I pray for dependence on Him for guidance; if each day I confess, restore, and renew my commitment to Him; and if each day I renew my mind with His truth, then I know that "he who began a good work in ... [me] will carry it on to completion until the day of Christ Jesus" (Philippians 1:6). It is up to me to believe that promise.

APPLY Paul is reminding the Philippians of truth he had told them before. Make a plan today for how you will daily remind yourself of the truths that will lead you to spiritual maturity.

_____

_____

_____

APPLY What things in your life will reflect that you are not a citizen of this world, but of heaven?

_____

_____

_____

Responding to Scripture

Summarize in your own words Paul's primary theme in Philippians 3:16–20a.

_____

_____

_____

_____

Responding to Life

In what area of your life could you most readily apply Paul's message in these verses?

_____

_____

_____

_____

Responding to God

 Dear heavenly Father, thank You for attaining salvation for me through the life, death, and resurrection of Your Son Jesus Christ. Thank You for calling me to share in what He has done. I also thank You for the examples of saints who have gone before me who have modeled a life of faithfulness for me to follow. Please help me to live as faithfully and encourage those who might one day look at my life as a source of encouragement in Christ. Father, most of all, help me to live as a faithful citizen of heaven while on earth—to inspire others to know how they can become citizens of heaven as well. In Christ's name I pray. Amen.

PROMISE OF GLORIFICATION (PHILIPPIANS 3:20–4:1)

When we become believers in Christ, our citizenship (our true home) is in heaven. We live *in* this world but are not *of* it (Romans 12:2). Just as Philippi was a colony of Rome in Macedonia, Christians make up a colony of heaven on earth, and Paul is reminding them of this. We are pilgrims on earth, journeying toward our eternal home. Warren Wiersbe says, "Many times the laws of heaven conflict with the laws of earth, but our responsibility is to obey God, and not men." [14]

> "Doctrine is only the drawing of the bow; application is hitting the mark."
>
> **Thomas Manton**

CITIZENSHIP

Paul knew his audience. When he told the Philippians their citizenship was in heaven (Philippians 3:20), they would have caught his meaning immediately. Philippi was a prominent Roman colony in Macedonia, and the Philippians were Roman citizens with all the rights and benefits of citizenship. Being a Roman citizen actually saved Paul on one occasion (Acts 22:28). Roman citizens were proud of their citizenship, and the Philippians would have instantly transferred their understanding of citizenship to the idea of being citizens of heaven.

The problem is that not many of us truly understand what it means to be citizens of heaven. We don't know what heaven is like, and we don't know what it is to be part of God's kingdom now. However, if our entire life is dependent upon us knowing Christ, if our citizenship is with Him, if we are to bring others to Him, if His kingdom defines everything we are now and what we will become, it would be in our best interest to put more effort into learning what it will be like. As we eagerly await our Savior, we ought to learn and plan and pray and prepare for His coming. Jesus taught that we should pray, "your kingdom come; your will be done on earth as it is in heaven." So when we begin to bring the culture of God's kingdom into our world, we are actually bringing a little bit of heaven to earth like Jesus did. This is the task we are charged with.

OUR TRUE HOME

Many years ago, a man visited a long-time friend, a British military officer stationed in the jungle of Africa. One day when the friend entered the officer's hut, he was startled to see him dressed in formal attire, seated at a table beautifully set with silverware and fine china. The visitor, thinking his friend might have lost his mind, asked why he was all dressed up and seated at this sumptuous table out in the middle of nowhere. The officer explained, "Once a week I follow this routine to remind myself of who I am—a British citizen. I want to maintain the customs of my real home and live according to the codes of British conduct, no matter how those around me live. I want to avoid substituting a foreign culture for that of my homeland." [15]

Christians ought to have a similar concern for contemplating our true citizenship in heaven. We must be aware of substituting the foreign culture of this world for that of our real homeland. We are not to take on its sinful ways or adopt its values. We need to live in such a way that others will see we are different. But in order to do this, we must know what those differences should be. As children in a school for ex-patriots learn about the culture of their homeland, we also should be learning about the culture of heaven and representing it on earth. Searching for knowledge about our citizenship and about our King is an essential prerequisite to avoiding the sins of this world.

OUR TRUE BODIES

And we eagerly await a Savior from there, the Lord Jesus Christ, who, by the power that enables him to bring everything under his control, will transform our lowly bodies so that they will be like his glorious body. (Philippians 3:20b–21)

Our bodies will eventually represent our true citizenship as well. How many of us are unhappy with our bodies now? Of course, it only takes one visit to a hospital or a nursing home to remind you that if you can walk or talk without pain you are indeed blessed. After watching a mother with Alzheimer's and a father with Lou Gehrig's Disease, I have witnessed first-hand how painful a deteriorating body can be.

But it's not just our physical flesh we struggle with; our spiritual "flesh" can actually cause us far more pain. We lose sleep over anxious thoughts. We suffer heart attacks from self-induced stress. We are worn out from trying to make everyone happy and meeting all their needs.

But Paul brings us comfort when he says Christ will one day transform our bodies—both physical and spiritual. Just as our lives on this earth are temporary, so the bodies we live in are temporary too. Jesus will fashion us like His own body of glory. This begins to take place for all who believe in Jesus as their Savior. Spiritually speaking, their heaven begins on earth. By faith, their souls are being transformed, and their bodies will one day undergo such a renewal as to fit their regenerated spirits. We don't know how soon this will happen, but the thought that this promise awaits us should help us bear the trials of this body and the woes of the flesh.

What a glorious promise we have! Though we have stewardship of these bodies while on earth, there will be a time when there is no more worry about being thin enough, or pretty enough, or even healthy enough. No more struggles with inner conflict and turmoil. No more tears or pain or anger or loneliness. Paul brought a glorious promise to the Philippians to help them in their time of need. What a lifeline for us in the times we live! Whether in life or death, behold old things have gone away, and all things are new. When we enter into "glory," we are entering into God's presence and all that comes with it: a new home *and* a new body!

APPLY What practices or values do you maintain in your life, which are not reflective of the kingdom of heaven? What practices or values could you substitute in their place?

_____

_____

_____

_____

APPLY If you moved to a foreign country to live indefinitely, what would you need to learn to fit in? How does that compare with becoming a citizen of heaven? What have you had to learn to fit into the kingdom of God or to avoid fitting in too well in this world?

_____

_____

_____

_____

OUR TRUE HOPE

Therefore, my brothers, you whom I love and long for, my joy and crown, that is how you should stand firm in the Lord, dear friends! (Philippians 4:1)

Paul concludes with the command to "stand firm in the Lord." He reminds the Philippians never to forget who and whose they really are. They are not Philippians first, or Romans first, or even Macedonians. They are children of God and followers of Christ. He is their cornerstone, their rock, their foundation, and as the old hymn says, "all other ground is sinking sand."

The English name, Stephen, comes from the Greek word for crown, *stephanos*. In the first century it most often referred to a garland of leaves placed on the head of a victorious athlete (2 Timothy 2:5). The word was used in the New Testament to signify awards given by God to victorious Christians. More than one kind of crown is mentioned as forthcoming: a "crown of righteousness" (2 Timothy 4:8), a "crown of life" (James 1:12), and a "crown of glory" (1 Peter 5:4).

📖 Why did Paul consider the Philippians his "crown"?
(See 1 Thessalonians 2:19 for another use of the word "crown.")

_____

_____

_____

APPLY How are you making yourself able to stand "in the Lord"? What defenses do you have in place to keep your foundation in Him from being shaken?

_____

_____

_____

_____

_____

Responding to Scripture

What is Paul's main theme or message in Philippians 3:20b—4:1?

_____

_____

_____

_____

Responding to Life

What positive difference would it make if you applied these words to your life?

_____

_____

_____

_____

_____

Responding to God

 Dear heavenly Father, thank You that You have made me a citizen of heaven through faith in Christ. I pray the values of heaven would be evident in my life during my time on this earth. I pray those who know me would recognize I am from a "foreign country," that I am living in this world but not *of* this world. I look forward to dwelling in heaven in the presence of Jesus Christ, and I pray You will help me to stand firm in that hope. In Christ's name I pray. Amen.

REVIEW FOR FOLLOWING GOD

If you ignored preparation and tried to run a marathon, you'd most likely injure yourself. Instead, you would make a plan, buy some sweat gear, maybe a new pair of sneakers, and start slowly, and more importantly, intentionally. Most Christians don't apply this principle to their spiritual lives. Instead, they are fooled into thinking they will just grow into mature, consistent followers of Christ over time, without any preparation or degree of intentionality.

In John Ortberg's book on the subject of spiritual disciplines, *The Life You've Always Wanted*, he shares how some Christians are "trying" to grow in the Christian life, while others are "training" for growth:

> *What does it mean to enter training? It means to arrange your life around certain exercises and experiences that will enable you to do eventually what you are not yet able to do even by trying hard. Training is essential for almost any significant endeavor in life, whether running a marathon, becoming a surgeon, or learning to play the piano. The need for preparation or training does not stop when it comes to learning the art of forgiveness, joy, or courage. It applies to a vibrant spiritual life just as it does to other activities. Learning to think, feel, and act like Jesus is at least as demanding as learning to run a marathon or play the piano. Maybe more so.*

> *To follow Jesus means learning to arrange our lives around those practices that will enable us to stay connected to Him and live more and more like Him.* [16]

REVIEW OF DAY 1: PRESSING ON TOWARD THE GOAL (PHILIPPIANS 3:12–13)

Any successful business executive will tell you the same thing: always start with a vision. We've all heard the tales of billion dollar ideas drawn on restaurant napkins. That is vision. The success of your Christian walk doesn't revolve around how difficult it is, how much you pray, or how much you tithe. To a large degree, success in your faith is determined by how much you follow the vision God has given you for each day.

One thing to remember is that God has put specific desires and needs in your heart. Your specific call will fulfill those longings. Though it is really God's vision, you were created for that call. Keeping your mind on Christ and His help will keep you humble enough to remain sharp and focused.

So, just as with running a race, start small and build up. Today it begins with you being intentional, and tomorrow you will try to achieve the goals you set today. Perhaps it's praying for thirty minutes during your day. Perhaps it's reaching out to someone. You probably have a good idea already of where to start. If not, ask the Holy Spirit. Once you're off and running, don't look back. Keep running and keep pressing on no matter what. You can't fathom how much the Lord can use a humble, intentional heart.

APPLY What is one thing you can do to become more intentional about your faith? How do you think it will affect you once that becomes part of your life?

Did You Know?
STARTING SMALL

When the Jewish captives returned from Persia to Jerusalem to rebuild the temple, they had to build "from scratch" in the face of much opposition. The Lord said through the prophet Zechariah, "Who despises the day of small things? Men will rejoice when they see the plumb line in the hand of Zerubbabel" (Zechariah 4:10). Rebuilding the temple would only happen one stone at a time. Building a mature spiritual life happens the same way.

_____

_____

_____

_____

REVIEW OF DAY 2: THE PRIZE OF PERSISTENCE (PHILIPPIANS 3:14–15)

All important endeavors require both short-term and long-term goals. Paul talks about focusing on the ultimate prize of our heavenward call to meet our Lord Jesus. He also mentions pressing onward to the end. Finishing strong simply means having fought well (having done your best) every day. Start today and purpose in your heart to finish this day well, doing your best. Keep doing that, and soon you will look back and be amazed at how far you've come.

At the end of the day, there is really only one goal we need to focus on: our relationship with Jesus Christ. When we focus on building our relationship with Him a little every day, we begin to have breakthroughs in our lives. In some cases, things that have seemed impossible for years will suddenly fall into place. You build your relationship with Christ through prayer and discovering his nature through His Word. When you do that every day, you will discover the prize that persistence offers—transformation into His image.

Do you think Jesus had goals? Are there Scriptures that show the answer? How might his approach to goals affect your life?

_____

_____

_____

_____

REVIEW OF DAY 3: HOW TO LIVE (PHILIPPIANS 3:16–20A)

So many of us talk a great spiritual game. We know the buzzwords: the hallelujahs, the glory bes, the anointings falling down on us. But what happens when we step out of the church building? Or if we're at an office luncheon and someone tells an off-color joke? Do we recoil at the thought of being shunned and go along with it? Or do we simply remove ourselves, or better yet, say you find the joke offensive so they'll know better next time?

We're not called to judge each other, but we are called to help each other grow. The best way to do that is to use the only measuring stick we need: Jesus. He attained freedom, victory, hope, and joy. Are we living like Him? The key is remaining consistent. Peter used the word "alert." He tells us to remain on guard, or alert, because the devil walks around as a roaring lion, looking for weak people whom he can devour (1 Peter 5:8). Don't be weak. Don't give up an inch to the enemy. Live up to what has been attained for you, and you will live life victoriously.

Many of us, however, tend to put off preparing for heaven until a time in the future. We think we have at least a _little_ leeway—time to think, time to plan, time to figure out how God fits into our lives. The problem with that mentality is that it can rob us of so much progress. We get tricked into being earthly minded when Paul clearly reminds us our citizenship is in heaven.

We are just passing through, so why waste a day on earthly pursuits that aren't pleasing to God?

Again, when we focus on a daily relationship with Christ and invite the Holy Spirit to fill us (Ephesians 5:18), we establish bulwarks against the enemy—strong fortresses that are impregnable and retain the fire of the Holy Spirit. Each day we will burn brighter.

APPLY Jesus has already attained victory for us; we have essentially won the battle and the war. If you are not seeing victory in your life, can you identify what might be disrupting your claim on what has been attained for you?

_____

_____

_____

_____

REVIEW OF DAY 4: GLORIOUS NEW BODIES (PHILIPPIANS 3:20—4:1)

If our citizenship is in heaven, surely we'll need new bodies. Indeed, we will, and our bodies will be something special. We don't know exactly what they'll look like, but Paul tells us we'll be like Jesus. Jesus said He goes before us to prepare a place for us. Three times in the New Testament, our earthly body is referred to as a tent (2 Corinthians 5:1, 4; 2 Peter 1:13). So if Jesus said He was going to prepare rooms for us (John 14:2), and our earthly bodies are mere tents, that tells us our heavenly bodies are going to be more substantial.

Toward this goal, we must honor the Lord with our earthly bodies and live our lives on earth as the temporary occupants we are. We are not here permanently, and we should not put up residence here. We should never let the culture of this world rub off on us, and we should never, ever conform to this world's ways. Instead, we work with what we have, our tents, and serve the Lord with them. We focus on our heavenly home and the astounding beauty and pleasure it will contain for us. That makes the temporary inconveniences we face in this world more bearable.

📖 What promises does God make to us regarding endurance and spiritual maturity? Read Romans 5:3–4. How can this motivate you to overcome every day?

_____

_____

_____

_____

"Our bodies shall be like Christ's glorious body, not equal to it."

Richard Sibbes

REVIEW PHILIPPIANS 3:12–21

Review the Scriptures and content of this week's lessons and identify three ideas, themes, or action points that struck you from what you studied this week. Especially look for ideas to apply to your own life.

1. _____

_____

_____

2. _____
_____
_____
_____

3. _____
_____
_____
_____
_____

REFLECT ON PHILIPPIANS 3:12

> *Not that I have already obtained all this, or have already been made perfect, but I press on to take hold of that for which Christ Jesus took hold of me.*

How do you see yourself emulating Jesus when you take hold of a new milestone in your faith walk?

_____
_____
_____
_____
_____
_____
_____
_____
_____

REMEMBER GOD'S GRACE IN YOUR LIFE

 Heavenly Father, thank You for this week's study on spiritual maturity. I ask You to help me understand how to grow effectively and with deep, healthy roots planted in our Lord Jesus Christ. I pray You help me to see daily the goal of my upward call to heaven, but also help me to take as many people with me as possible. Please help me to honor You with my life as I work out my salvation in Christ Jesus, with the help of the Holy Spirit. In Jesus' name I pray. Amen.

Philippians 4:2-9

LESSON OVERVIEW

EXHORTATION

Paul encouraged the Philippians to guard their minds. The possibility of rejoicing only comes with the practice of proper thinking. Whether faced with disagreements among themselves or anxiety due to their circumstances, the Philippians needed to understand that joy could only be found through faith in the promises of God.

Paul did not give the Philippians a "to do" list, but rather a "to think" list. How often do I write down what I need to get done in a day? Yet how much more do I need to pay attention to what I think? Paul reminds Christians they need to do the real work of putting their minds in the right place.

If I think I have to meet everyone's needs, that life is spinning out of control, and I'm completely helpless, my mind is to blame. My anxiety is a problem of thoughts, not circumstances.

But if I think about the love and power of Christ who dwells within me, that my circumstances are under His control, that I have nothing to fear because He is there with me every step of the way, then my mind will think properly. I will think and walk in the truth.

Philippians 4:2-9

PROBLEMS OF DISUNITY (PHILIPPIANS 4:2-3)

Did You Know?

DENOMINATIONS

According to the World Christian Encyclopedia (2001) there are 38,000 Christian denominations in the world.

> "As soon as the love of God was shed abroad in my soul I loved all, of whatever denomination, who loved the Lord Jesus in sincerity of heart."
>
> **George Whitefield**

Paul's pre-conversion life put him in a unique position for ministry. The Pharisee sect of Judaism into which Paul was born was the strictest order of all the Jewish religious groups. Paul excelled in this sect and was blameless in keeping the Mosaic Law and traditions of the Pharisees.

An exclusive religious group, the Pharisees looked down on anyone who wasn't one of them. Those who didn't meticulously adhere to the tiniest details of the law were considered unclean and filthy sinners. During Paul's training, it may have been his goal to attain the revered position of High Priest over all of Israel's priests. He studied under Gamaliel, the most renowned teacher of the law (Acts 22:3) and a Hebrew prodigy.

Upon his conversion to Christ, Paul immediately became an outcast among the religious elite of Israel, even having a bounty placed on his life. As if that weren't enough, he was sent by God to the Gentiles—the unbelieving, "unclean" people with whom the Pharisees wouldn't even shake hands.

Paul's background made him all too familiar with the destructive potential of religious disagreements and division.

STRESS ON LEADERS

> *I plead with Euodia and I plead with Syntyche to agree with each other in the Lord. (Philippians 4:2)*

There are times we might think certain passages of Scripture are dated and not applicable to modern times. This is understandable given how long ago the Bible was written. In this passage, however, we see that even in the early years of the New Testament church, there were striking similarities to our present-day church. Differences and disagreements had already surfaced. Paul's words in this short verse speak volumes to us today. His tone is distressed, while he clearly begs these two prominent church leaders to agree with each other. Paul suggests these women make Christ the sole focus of their *unity* instead of the cause for their *disagreement*.

Fast forward two thousand years. How many denominations exist under the Christian banner today? While those differences may not be resolved before Christ returns, all Christians can unite around that which binds us together in Christ. Romans 10:9 says that if we confess Jesus as Lord and believe in our hearts that God raised Him from the dead, we will be saved. There are fundamental doctrines like the deity of Christ and His death and resurrection for the salvation of sinners that should unite all Christians, in spite of our differences, as we proclaim Him to a lost world.

How well have we done to agree with each other in the Lord? The key is focusing on what unites us, not what divides us.

The next time you are tempted to take pride in your own denominational (or non-denominational) status, remember that we all have Jesus in common.

We are all Christ followers who love our Lord dearly and equally. *That* is something we can agree on.

If all believers focused on the common elements within our faith communities, how might that impact the Great Commission (Matthew 28:19–20)?

_____

_____

_____

 What common elements of the faith does your church or denomination share with others in your community that could serve as the basis for unity?

_____

_____

_____

SUPPORT FOR LEADERS

> *Yes, and I ask you, loyal yokefellow, help these women who have contended at my side in the cause of the gospel, along with Clement and the rest of my fellow workers, whose names are in the book of life. (Philippians 4:3)*

There are two interesting details to note in this verse. First, Paul makes a point of commending these two women who have contended (done battle) at his side for the cause of the Gospel. Adding to our denominational differences is the role of women in the church, which has been a topic of debate from the early church until now. Even Paul had some interesting things to say about this topic at certain times of his ministry. What is evident, however, is these two women, who were clearly leaders in their church communities, were invaluable to Paul and had done much to further the Gospel.

Secondly, Paul instructs his "loyal yokefellow" (fellow servant of the Gospel) to help these women in their ongoing mission to spread the message of Christ despite their disagreements. It is clear from Philippians 4:2 there was some contention between the two "camps" of Euodia and Syntyche, but Paul highlights two things: everyone was on the same team, and they were all working toward a common goal of spreading the Gospel.

Paul first addresses how the leaders should focus on agreeing together in the Lord, and then he goes on to instruct those supporting the leaders to help them despite any contention.

It is human nature to have opinions—to take sides in disagreements. But this can have a devastating effect on our unity with others. Unity is essential for the higher goal of spreading the Gospel. Paul had lived through sectarianism, being a Pharisee and a son of a Pharisee (Acts 23:6). His entire life up to his conversion had been focused on the superiority of the Pharisaical doctrine—on taking sides against those who disagreed. He was in a unique position to say petty disagreements would do nothing to advance their cause as a unified church.

Paul was asking these men and women to submit their time and resources to help these two *women* with the ultimate goal of spreading the Gospel.

Did You Know?
UNITY

A famous quotation about unity has been mis-attributed to St. Augustine of Hippo, though it is not found in his writings. Regardless of its source, it stands as a benchmark by which to measure disagreements: "Unity in necessary things; liberty in doubtful things; charity in all things." The primary weakness in the rule is that people do not always agree on what is "necessary" versus what is "doubtful." Two well-known Christian denominations—the Moravian Church and the Evangelical Presbyterian Church (United States) have adopted the rule as a motto.

Word Study
LOYAL YOKEFELLOW

Scholars are not sure whether Paul is addressing an unnamed individual or a person named Suzygus since the word appears in the midst of three other proper nouns. The Greek word, *suzuge*, could be translated as a proper noun (name) or as a reference to an unnamed individual.

> "Unity in Christ is not something to be achieved; it is something to be recognized."
>
> A. W. Tozer

Forget about disagreements in doctrine; roll up your sleeves and work. He also reminds them of the reward of having their names written in the Lamb's Book of Life.

📖 What do you think may have led to the lack of help among the community Paul is addressing? (Philippians 4:3)

_____

_____

_____

APPLY Have you ever been distracted from spreading the Gospel? What do you think caused the distraction? Can you identify a remedy in this passage of Scripture?

_____

_____

_____

_____

Responding to Scripture

In your own words, describe Paul's big idea in Philippians 4:2–3.

_____

_____

_____

_____

_____

Responding to Life

What difference would it make if you applied his teaching in your life?

_____

_____

_____

_____

Responding to God

 Dear heavenly Father, I know I have been involved in disagreements with others over trivial matters, and I ask your forgiveness. I know a testimony of love among Your people is the most important part of spreading the gospel. I pray You will help me be a loving person even if I have a disagreement over a trivial matter. Please help me preserve the unity of Your people and build up the body of Christ. In Christ's name I pray. Amen.

PRAYERS AND PETITIONS (PHILIPPIANS 4:4–6)

Paul re-emphasizes his message to the Philippians: "Rejoice in the Lord always" (Philippians 4:4). When I first heard this phrase, I wasn't really sure what it meant. Did it mean to rejoice in the Lord all day long, or perhaps, that every day we should be happy and bubbly, never allowing ourselves to be sad? The latter seemed impossible. When I was going through a severe trial, anyone who tried to force me to be happy and bubbly at that time could be profoundly annoying or even harmful. So how does one rejoice always, no matter what we're going through?

HOW TO REJOICE ALWAYS

> *Rejoice in the Lord always. I will say it again: Rejoice! Let your gentleness be evident to all. The Lord is near. (Philippians 4:4–5)*

Understanding of the Bible often happens when the Bible explains itself by combining insights from several verses or passages. With regard to rejoicing, Habakkuk 3:17–18 says:

> *Though the fig tree does not bud*
> *and there are no grapes on the vines,*
> *though the olive crop fails*
> *and the fields produce no food,*
> *though there are no sheep in the pen*
> *and no cattle in the stalls,*
> *yet I will rejoice in the LORD,*
> *I will be joyful in God my Savior.*

Obviously, Habakkuk was no stranger to difficulties. In this case, he faced starvation and the triumph of evil all around him, yet he didn't stop rejoicing. His secret lay in the word "Savior." Some translations read, "I will be joyful in the God of my salvation." The word "salvation" has connotations of provision, healing, restoration, and strength. Habakkuk discovered a joy that did not depend on surrounding circumstances, but instead, on his hope of a future salvation and in the character of the one who would save him. This is not a joy a person manufactures, but it is one we can ask for (Read Psalm 51:12).

Note that Habakkuk is contrasting his struggles with rejoicing in the Lord's salvation. This is important, because it emphasizes salvation doesn't mean freedom from all struggles.

The original Greek word for "gentleness" in the phrase "let your gentleness be evident to all" (Philippians 4:5) can also be translated as "patience." This means patience is required through tough times, even while still rejoicing. When you think about it, we wouldn't need salvation if we didn't go through struggles, an insight one minister called "spiritual common sense."

Here's another angle to consider. In her book *If I Live to Be 100,* author and National Public Radio host, Neenah Ellis, interviewed more than twenty-five

Doctrine
REJOICE IN THE LORD

As an expert of the Old Testament, Paul often incorporated language from those books in his New Testament epistles. For example, the phrase "rejoice in the Lord" occurs ten times in the Old Testament:

Psalm 32:11

Psalm 35:9

Psalm 64:10

Psalm 97:12

Psalm 104:34

Isaiah 29:19

Isaiah 41:16

Joel 2:23

Habakkuk 3:18

Zechariah 10:7

Its two occurrences in the New Testament are both in Philippians: 3:1 and 4:4.

An exhortation similar to "rejoice always" is found in I Thessalonians 5:18: "Give thanks in all circumstances." This seems just as counterintuitive as rejoicing always. But Paul doesn't say to give thanks for all circumstances, but in all circumstances. In the midst of any circumstance the Christian is able to give thanks to God. Why? Because God has promised to cause all things to work together for good in the lives of those who love Him (Romans 8:28).

> **"It is the very joy of this earthly life to think that it will come to an end."**
>
> **Charles Spurgeon**

centenarians. Every one of them said that what keeps them going is having something to look forward to. The writer of Hebrews puts it this way when explaining how Jesus endured the suffering of the cross:

> *Let us fix our eyes on Jesus, the author and perfecter of our faith, who for the joy set before him endured the cross, scorning its shame, and sat down at the right hand of the throne of God. (Hebrews 12:2)*

It was the "joy set before him" that allowed Jesus to endure the suffering of the cross. "Let us fix our eyes on Jesus" clearly suggests we are to imitate him. If the joy of accomplishing the Father's will and sitting down at God's right hand allowed Jesus to persevere, then looking forward to heaven with Him can do the same for us.

APPLY How might patience and joy go hand in hand? Can you think of a time when you had to exercise both? On what or to whom did you "fix your eyes"?

_____

_____

_____

_____

APPLY What do you have to look forward to? When weighed against your trials, which seems greater?

_____

_____

_____

HANDING YOUR ANXIETY OVER TO GOD

> *Do not be anxious about anything, but in everything, by prayer and petition, with thanksgiving, present your requests to God. (Philippians 4:6)*

There was a man who lived some time ago and at times suffered from extreme anxiety. When he was nine years old, the man's mother died. Growing up on a farm he had only about eighteen total months of formal education. He tried his hand at business in his early twenties but failed. He then tried his hand at politics and failed again. By the time he was twenty-four, he tried again at business—only to fail again.

Life brightened for the young man when he fell deeply in love with a wonderful young lady and was looking forward to marrying her. She died of typhoid fever. He spiraled into a period of deep depression and suffered what we now call a mental breakdown. He eventually got over this tragedy, and eight years later he entered a Congressional race. He lost. Two years later he tried again and lost again. Over the next thirteen years he would lose another two senatorial races and an attempt to run for vice president. The man was known for having chronic anxiety to the point of doubting his sanity. At fifty-two years of age this man became the sixteenth president of the United States. You may have already guessed this man was Abraham Lincoln.

If you're wondering how President Lincoln was able to face such adversity while suffering from anxiety and depression, some clues can be gleaned from his speeches. Below are two that stand out to me:

"I turn, then, and look to the American people and to that God who has never forsaken them." [Address to the Ohio Legislature on February 13, 1861]

"Intelligence, patriotism, Christianity, and a firm reliance on Him, who has never yet forsaken this favored land, are still competent to adjust, in the best way, all our present difficulty." [First Inaugural Address on March 4, 1861]

President Lincoln knew a secret. No matter what life threw at him, he believed God was in control. He knew how to commit everything through prayer to God. The result was not a perfect life, but he had the ability to possess peace and confidence in the middle of difficult times.

APPLY Have you ever felt better after talking a problem through with someone? What difference does it make after discussing your problems with God? And how exactly do you do this?

_____

_____

_____

_____

How does the Holy Spirit act as a resource of strength and patience in your life? (Galatians 5:22–23)

_____

_____

_____

_____

A petition usually contains a subject for consideration. How might that be significant in light of this Scripture (Philippians 4:6)?

_____

_____

_____

Responding to Scripture

How would you describe the Apostle Paul's main point in Philippians 4:4–6?

_____

_____

_____

_____

Responding to Life

What would be the most immediate way for you to apply this teaching to your life?

_____

_____

Doctrine
JESUS AND PAUL

We only have one written example of Paul quoting Jesus (Acts 20:35). That is not surprising, since Paul was not a disciple of Jesus during His earthly ministry. But Paul's words in Philippians 4:6 are a capsule summary of Jesus' teaching in the Sermon on the Mount about worry and anxiety (Matthew 6:25–34). Jesus told His followers to commit all their needs and cares to God—exactly what Paul recommended in Philippians 4:6.

"The beginning of anxiety is the end of faith, and the beginning of true faith is the end of anxiety."

George Müller

_____

_____

_____

Responding to God

 Dear heavenly Father, thank You for making it possible for me to rejoice in You at all times. Even though I am still learning how to choose to be joyful in every circumstance, thank You for making it possible. Please help me to grow in my ability to find joy in you and not in my circumstances. Help me, Lord, to remember to commit everything to You in prayer, with thanksgiving, and trust You with the outcome of every prayer. In Christ's name I pray. Amen.

Philippians 4:2-9

DAY THREE

PEACE OF GOD (PHILIPPIANS 4:7)

Word Study

PEACE

Scholars believe the Greek word for peace (eirene—note the basis for the female name, Irene) comes from a word meaning "to join." Therefore, peace with an enemy is to join in cessation of hostility; peace with God means to join with God in settling the issue of sin. Peace in Philippians 4:6 is the peace of God which flows from peace with God (Romans 5:1). It is the peace Paul writes about in Romans 15:13: *"joy and peace in believing, that you may abound in hope. . ." (KJV).*

Missy, our middle daughter, was a cautious child. She always made sure the doors were locked in our house, and when we walked down the streets or through the malls, she stayed far away from strangers. But I remember one place where Missy was a Wonder Woman of courage.

A swimming pool in our neighborhood had two diving boards—a low board and a really high one. When Missy was around seven years old, she would barely walk out to the end of the low board. But eventually, with her daddy treading water beneath the end of the board, she would jump off into his arms. Daddy's outstretched arms were all she needed to exchange caution for courage. It wasn't long before my husband, Terry, moved to the side of the pool from beneath the end of the board, and then out of the pool to a deck chair—all the while in plain sight. That's all Missy needed to know; her daddy was there if she needed him.

It was no time before she was able to run, jump, and dive off the end of the board–even doing a backflip. When Missy moved to the high board, she ran the same test. Is Daddy there? Check. Off she went. She even did backflips off the high board, causing everybody at the pool, including me, to gasp when she flipped. We would hold our combined breath until she surfaced. It was the presence of her dad that made the difference and allowed Missy to have peace where she had only known fear before.

I think that was the same reason the Apostle Paul was able to live a life of peace in the midst of fearful circumstances. He knew his heavenly Father was there. He knew God was in control and was there if Paul needed him. Therefore, Paul had peace—the kind of peace only God can give.

WHAT IS REAL PEACE?

And the peace of God, which transcends all understanding. (Philippians 4:7a)

Many times the subtle meanings of popular idioms get lost in their overuse. Take for example the phrase, "She can't see the forest for the trees." Most of us have used this idiom when referring to someone who is so close to a problem she can't see the bigger picture; she gets bogged down in the details. In a business context, this can lead to slight, but critical changes in focus, which can eventually translate into missing the objective in a major way. While this is a good use of the idiom, another perspective I like relates to a Scripture you might have heard before:

> "*As the heavens are higher than the earth, so are my ways higher than your ways and my thoughts than your thoughts.*" (Isaiah 55:9)

We know God only wants good for us in the same way we want only good for our children (Luke 11:11–13). So if God's ways are higher than our ways, as the heavens are higher than the earth, then surely when it comes to worrying about our lives we're seeing the trees instead of the forest. If God's ways are higher than ours, surely he has a bigger plan for us that we don't understand. If we worry about the details of the trials we face, and even worry about *why* we're going through them, how will we ever be able to focus on fulfilling God's plans for us?

Real peace transcends our understanding, and this is the secret Paul understood and clung to. This secret was indeed the key to enduring those severe trials he faced. God's ways are higher than ours. Unless we're derailing God's plans for us through intentional sin, God *will* bring about good in our lives whether we understand what is going on or not. That fact is more certain than the guarantee the sun will rise tomorrow. Yes, we will face trials, especially when we start living intentionally for God. But God has promised to bring about good in our lives and as a *result* of our lives as well. We don't have to worry about a thing.

If you're going through trials at the moment, think about God's promises. Even if your life is weighed down or off-track due to your own choices or sin, God can heal every situation.

First, you need to gain peace by believing He will bring good to you. Then you won't be tempted to make irrational decisions based on worry. In fact, God's peace will rise above your mind's understanding, allowing you to see the big picture that He will ultimately bring good to your life.

📖 How did Peter describe God's promises in 2 Peter 1:3–4? What do we "participate" in if we cling to them?

_____

_____

_____

📖 What do you learn about God's "ways" from Romans 8:28?

_____

_____

_____

_____

"*Grace is the free favour of God; peace is the condition which results from its reception.*"

H. L. Goudge

> ***"The gem cannot be polished without friction, nor man perfected without trials."***
>
> **Anonymous**

In Isaiah 55:10–11, what do those verses suggest about the result of God's "ways" in your life? How does that apply to going through trials?

_____

_____

_____

_____

GOD'S PEACE IS A GUARDIAN

Will guard your hearts and your minds in Christ Jesus. (Philippians 4:7b)

Our minds are always being fed, either by default or by discipline. If we do nothing, we let the world feed our minds with its lies and deceptions. If we discipline ourselves to hear God's Word, we feed our minds with the truth of God's love and experience His peace.

I will never forget one summer I decided not to feed (guard) my mind at all. In fact, it had been a busy year of teaching my Bible study, so I decided to "take a break" that summer and do nothing. I mean nothing. I just read magazines at the beach, watched TV, did a little shopping—you get the idea. As those three months went by, however, I noticed my attitude beginning to change little by little. I began to panic as I rushed from place to place. I began to worry about things like my appearance and being accepted by others. I took to heart the slightest sarcastic comment my friends or family members made and was overly sensitive. In fact, a whole array of insignificant issues became cataclysmic.

Then, as the summer was ending, it was time to start teaching again. As I took out my Bible, I began to weep. It was as though God was saying through His Word, "Where have you been, Nancy? You know all these things you are worried about are so unimportant. All that matters is your relationship with me, and I love you just as you are." I renewed my commitment at that moment to always "guard my mind," to stay in God's Word. For his truth will always stand guard over our hearts.

Today's Scripture tells us something quite interesting. It says the peace of God will guard our hearts and minds in Christ Jesus. So not only when our hearts and minds are guarded do we have peace, but it is the *peace of God* that guards our hearts and minds. This is a simple, but profound, truth. It means when we submit to God, we hand over our cares to Him through prayer and requests, and then the peace that transcends our mind's limits will completely fill us. This peace acts as a guardian in the strength of Jesus Christ against any imitation relief we are tempted to seek. It may be as simple as the fear of what others think or just being super-sensitive. It could be gossip. It could be flirting with the boss at work despite the ring on his finger. Anything outside of Christ Jesus, however, will lead to ruin. God's peace will protect our hearts and minds vigilantly and effectively.

APPLY Can you identify what often causes you to lose your peace? Can you see a pattern anywhere in that process?

_____

_____

_____

___

___

📖 What does Isaiah 26:3 say happens to the person whose mind stays centered on God? Why does it happen?

___

___

___

Responding to Scripture

Summarize in your own words what Paul is saying in Philippians 4:7.

___

___

___

___

___

Responding to Life

What could happen in your life today if you applied what Paul teaches in this verse?

___

___

___

___

___

Responding to God

 Dear heavenly Father, thank You for the promise that I can have peace through committing all of my concerns to You. Thank You for promising to stand watch over my heart and my mind in Christ. Forgive me, Father, for the times I fail to commit everything to You, for the times I allow temptation and my choices to overcome Your promises to me. I ask that the Holy Spirit would continue to remind me to commit all my concerns to You in prayer so I can know Your peace. I pray in Christ's name. Amen.

PROPER THINKING (PHILIPPIANS 4:8–9)

Today, we hear so much about the mind and the power of positive thinking. While there is some truth to the many celebrity quotes that claim the benefits of positive thinking, nothing can give you a

📖 **Doctrine**
THE FRUIT OF THE SPIRIT

Peace, Paul writes, is the fruit of the Holy Spirit living in the believer's life (Galatians 5:22–23). The fruit of the Spirit are simply the character traits of Jesus Christ living in the Christian by the presence of the Spirit (Galatians 2:20). Christ lived a life of peace (John 14:27) and His peace is manifested through the Christian who does not grieve the Spirit by sin (Ephesians 4:30).

Philippians 4:2-9

DAY FOUR

> **"One of the highest and noblest functions of a man's mind is to listen to God's Word, and so to read his mind and think his thoughts after him."**
>
> **John R. W. Stott**

better outlook on life than the Word of God. Positive thinking–*proper* thinking–is simply *believing* what His Word says.

In fact, God takes offense when we don't believe what His Word says we can do. Consider the case of the twelve spies Moses sent to scope out the Promised Land (Numbers 13 and 14). All twelve reported the land flowed with milk and honey and that it was full of giants, but only Caleb and Joshua believed God would give them the power to defeat the enemies and take the land.

The remaining ten saw themselves as grasshoppers in the sight of the occupying giants and were too afraid to give the go-ahead. This resulted in fear spreading like a disease throughout the Israelite ranks and almost resulted in Caleb and Joshua being stoned to death. The difference between the ten other spies and Caleb and Joshua was that Caleb and Joshua saw themselves through the eyes of God. Whatever He said, they believed they could do. Needless to say, the ten spies died without entering the Promised Land, but Caleb and Joshua led the successful invasion thirty-eight years later.

THE MIND MAKES REALITY

> *Finally, brothers, whatever is true, whatever is noble, whatever is right, whatever is pure, whatever is lovely, whatever is admirable–if anything is excellent or praiseworthy–think about such things. (Philippians 4:8)*

You have no doubt heard the expression of "looking at life through rose-colored glasses"–an expression that simply means some people see a situation as better than it really is.

Scripture has a similar, but infinitely more true and powerful, effect as rose-colored glasses. You can take most circumstances in your life and find a promise regarding that problem. When you frame your circumstance in the light of the Word and fulfill the requirements of the promise, the new perspective will give you peace and hope.

This applies to seeing people through God's eyes too–seeing them as He sees them (John 13:34). What a difference we'd see in our home life if we only saw the good in others. It does not mean their behavior is perfect, but our perception of them can put things in proper perpective. If we focused on the good in others, I believe in our eyes, our husbands would soon transform into Godly knights in shining armor, and our children would become blessed little angels. This is what Paul means when he says, "think about such things."

If we looked at the world through the lens of Scripture, praising God for every good and perfect gift he daily brings our way, how much would our vision change? How about our lives? Why doesn't this come easily for us? The reason is, due to our fallen nature of sin, we're *naturally* pessimists. Our minds are darkened by the negative consequences of disobedience to God, and we can often only see the negative. Because humankind has missed the mark so often and for so long, it is difficult without God's help to escape that vicious cycle. But we can escape.

God lives in infinite light, love, and peace. He has all the answers. One of them is only thinking good, wholesome thoughts. Even when circumstances are going badly, think about things that are pure, true, lovely, noble, praiseworthy, and admirable. Think about your enemy's good qualities, and you'll discover compassion. Think about the character of Christ, and you'll discover humility. Keep a Godly attitude, and it will open doors for more peace. Even when you can't muster the ability to do these things, ask God for help, and He will supply it.

APPLY Can you remember a time when you had to admit you were completely wrong in assessing a situation? How could the outcome have been different if you trusted in positive intentions?

_____

_____

_____

If we fed our minds with God's unconditional love for us, how would that change the way we view others (John 13:34)?

_____

_____

_____

_____

PRACTICE MAKES PERFECT

Whatever you have learned or received or heard from me, or seen in me—put it into practice. And the God of peace will be with you. (Philippians 4:9)

There was a recent study on how long it takes a new habit to feel automatic in your daily routine. A researcher named Phillipa Lally from University College in London gathered data on eighty-four participants who added new habits to their daily routines: sit-ups, drinking a glass of water with lunch, going for a fifteen-minute run. Not surprisingly, the time for the habit to become automatic varied significantly for each participant. What was clear though, was for those who performed the behavior more consistently, the habit became automated more quickly. On average, it took the participants sixty-six days to develop a sense of automation in the behavior.

The Scripture above is simple. Paul says whatever we have learned from him or seen him do, put it into practice. Just do it, and the God of peace will be with you. For some of us, it will take a bit longer. For others, we'll see results in virtually no time. For all of us, thinking on good things and putting Christ-modeled behavior into practice guarantees that God—and His perfect peace—will be with us. It's an easy concept. We just need to do it.

APPLY What is the most difficult part of developing a good habit? How could you overcome this hurdle?

_____

_____

_____

_____

People often say certain tasks such as gardening give them a sense of peace. Do you believe there is a certain peace in doing, as opposed to thinking

Put Yourself in Their Shoes
EXAMPLES

The Apostle Paul was not hesitant to recommend that new Christians imitate his life and practices (1 Corinthians 4:16; 2 Thessalonians 3:9). This was not boasting, but the result of him patterning his life after Jesus Christ: "Follow my example, as I follow the example of Christ" (1 Corinthians 11:1). For first-century Christians who had not been around Christ during His three years on earth, Paul's life provided a pattern to follow. By imitating Paul, believers would be imitating Christ.

about what we should be doing? How could the two verses in today's Scripture be related in this way?

_____

_____

_____

_____

Responding to Scripture

Summarize in your own words the point Paul is making in Philippians 4:8–9.

_____

_____

_____

_____

_____

Responding to Life

In what area of your life can you most readily apply the lesson from this Scripture?

_____

_____

_____

_____

_____

Responding to God

 Dear heavenly Father, thank You for the promise of Your presence and Your peace. I know that practicing a godly lifestyle and thinking godly thoughts can have a powerful impact on my life. But I need the help of the Holy Spirit to make those choices today. I want to think thoughts that are pleasing to You and make choices that please You. I ask for Your help to think and act in the power of the Spirit. In Christ's name I pray. Amen.

Philippians 4:2-9

DAY FIVE

REVIEW FOR FOLLOWING GOD

When I'm at the beach, I often spot a flock of birds flying in their traditional "V" formation over the ocean, with one bird leading the charge. Many of us probably know the birds take turns at the front of the "V," but did you know there is an even more astounding reason for this phenomenon? A couple of engineers, studying a flock of geese, discovered that each bird, just by flapping its wings, creates an updraft of air for the birds behind. This creates a tremendous energetic advantage to the flock, allowing them to fly up to seventy percent further than if a bird was flying alone. [17]

In the same way, exhortation carries connotations of synergy—the whole creation of something greater than the sum of the parts. The more believers who successfully walk in unity, joy, peace, and proper thinking, the greater the effect we'll see within the church and upon our witness to the world.

REVIEW OF DAY 1: DISUNITY AND LEADERSHIP (PHILIPPIANS 4:2–3)

Disciples typically adopt their leaders' attitudes and sometimes, especially when our leaders are in disagreement, we may find ourselves having strained relationships with brothers and sisters in Christ. Leadership styles trickle down, and anyone in leadership will tell you it's usually not intentional, nor is it really avoidable. This means the culture of the pastor is usually replicated down the leadership hierarchy into the body, having a significant effect on the flock. This is why we need to pray so much for our leaders. They are fallible, and believe me, unless you are anointed for the work, you do not want their jobs, nor their accountability. This is why Paul encourages the Philippian leaders to put aside useless disagreements and then instructs the church to help their leadership and each other. Unity is the first step toward peace.

When you think about it, Christians are outnumbered by non-believers. Those of us who believe Jesus is the only begotten Son of God, who was raised from the dead, should be sticking together, no matter what. God will be able to do astounding things when that happens.

 APPLY What is one way you can practice greater unity in the Church? How can you commit to practicing this until it becomes a habit?

_____

_____

_____

REVIEW OF DAY 2: REJOICE (PHILIPPIANS 4:4–6)

It might seem strange to think in the middle of a difficult time that we should rejoice and be glad. Yet this is exactly what Paul is telling us to do in this passage of Scripture. Note he doesn't say "try to rejoice" or "if possible, rejoice." He says, "Rejoice in the Lord always." How do we do that, and more importantly, why should we? Because the Lord is near (Psalm 23:4) and will work things out for good to those who love Him (Romans 8:28). The truth that the Lord is near has implications that are easily overlooked. These implications are wrapped up in the word "salvation." Salvation means freedom from the past, provision for the present, and hope for the future. When that sinks in, you'll rejoice. But you need to spend time thinking about it in order for it to sink in.

It's no accident that Paul ties rejoicing together with overcoming anxiety. When viewed in light of the truth that the Lord is near and at work in your circumstance, it makes sense. Don't be anxious about anything, just make your requests to the Lord through prayer and with thanksgiving, because _He is near._ We give thanks because we know He hears us (John 11:41). Then we rejoice because he has everything under control. This is a significant step toward continuous peace and is truly encouraging.

"Happiness is caused by things that happen around me, and circumstances will mar it; but joy flows right on through trouble; joy flows on through the day; joy flows through persecution and opposition. It is an unceasing fountain bubbling up in the heart; a secret spring the world can't see and doesn't know anything about. The Lord gives his people perpetual joy when they walk in obedience to him."

Dwight L. Moody

What do you think might cause you to forget the Lord is near in your daily life? How could you build a greater awareness of His presence into your life?

_____

_____

_____

_____

REVIEW OF DAY 3: PEACE (PHILIPPIANS 4:7)

I believe there is a faulty expectation in much of the Western church. Probably because of our prosperity and comfortable modern lives we have come to believe a great lie that Scripture clearly contradicts. I believe this lie is at the root of much of our lack of peace. We expect to never be severely challenged in our faith.

Many people will say, "Oh, I know we're going to go through trials," but they fail to consider the severity of these challenges until they are in the midst of them. Consider, however, that the severity of your trials is frequently proportionate to the threat you pose to the enemy. Paul counted everything his meticulous religious education afforded him as garbage (Philippians 3:7). He was on a mission—heaven knew it, and hell knew it for sure. As a result, Paul suffered tremendously in ways I'm sure would cause most of those who claim to be believers today to quit. Eventually, Paul was martyred in prison, having gained such an understanding of Christ's worth he was more than happy to die for Christ (Acts 21:11–14). Paul had attained a peace that surpassed reason. How did he do that? Psalm 23:4 gives us the answer:

> *Even though I walk through the valley of the shadow of death, I will fear no evil, for you are with me; your rod and your staff, they comfort me.*

The short but profound answer is that Paul didn't just note the Lord was near. He clung to Christ. He filled his thoughts with Jesus and remained close to Him, and the Lord's presence in his life sustained him. He said God's grace was sufficient (2 Corinthians 12:9). You can have this unfathomable peace too. But first, you must come to expect persecution and related suffering and not give in to distress when it appears. This doesn't mean sickness, or trouble paying off the credit card. It means when you put yourself out on a limb to vocalize your faith, you will be persecuted. But God is right there on the limb with you.

 Why do you think that suffering for the Lord can actually bring about peace? How might the answer help you both endure suffering and attain a greater level of peace?

_____

_____

_____

_____

REVIEW OF DAY 4: PROPER THINKING (PHILIPPIANS 4:8–9)

This week, we learned that meditating on Scriptures and godly ideas can have a profound effect on our peace. When you view the world through the

> ## *"What we think about when we are free to think about what we will–that is what we are or will soon become."*
>
> ## *A. W. Tozer*

lens of Scripture, you can change your life. Have you ever considered that pessimism is akin to unbelief? What's even more important is that pessimists doubt God because they don't build their faith up on Scripture.

In the Scripture below, a father begs Jesus to cast a demon out of his son. The man was struggling with pessimism, and Jesus answers him in perfect love:

> *"If you can?" said Jesus. "Everything is possible for him who believes."*
> *Immediately the boy's father exclaimed, "I do believe; help me overcome my*
> *unbelief!" (Mark 9:23–24)*

How do you overcome unbelief? You fill your mind with godly thoughts and simply practice believing, no matter how awkward it may be at first. Start small and move up. Pretty soon, you'll realize the God of peace is with you, and you have nothing to fear.

APPLY How do you think the words of Jesus in Mark 9:23–24 about believing could affect your life? How would your life change if you could simply believe one hundred percent in God's power?

_____

_____

_____

_____

REVIEW PHILIPPIANS 4:2–9

Review the Scriptures and content of this week's lesson and identify three ideas, themes, or action points you would like to take from what you studied this week. Look especially for ideas to apply to your life.

1. _____

_____

_____

_____

2. _____

_____

_____

_____

3. _____

_____

_____

_____

REFLECTION ON PHILIPPIANS 4:9

> *Whatever you have learned or received or heard from me, or seen in me—*
> *put it into practice. And the God of peace will be with you.*

> **"One result of the unbelief of our day is the tragedy of trying to live a maximum life on a minimum faith."**
>
> *Rufus M. Jones*

What have you learned from Paul that you could put into practice in your own life?

_____

_____

_____

_____

_____

_____

REMEMBER GOD'S GRACE IN YOUR LIFE

 Heavenly Father, I thank You for this week's study on exhortation. Thank You that as a good Father You know how to encourage us. You raised up great teachers like the Apostle Paul to exhort us through Your Word. Please show me when I have opportunities to encourage others and build them up. Help me rejoice in trials and set an encouraging example. Help me achieve Your peace that surpasses understanding so I can be fully encouraged and hopeful to do Your work. I pray You will show me how to put into practice what I see in your Word. In Jesus precious name, I pray. Amen.

Philippians 4:10-23

LESSON OVERVIEW

EVERYTHING POSSIBLE THROUGH CHRIST

A poor farmer had a good year. One day he harvested everything he needed for his family to eat for a full day and took it to his wife to prepare. He went out and observed his garden, pleased with what God had given him. He laid down under the shade of a big walnut tree he had tended for years. He rested and thanked God for the nuts he would eat from it. He dozed off to sleep.

A rich man driving by saw the man sleeping and stopped to see if he was okay. He shook the poor man awake and asked if he was all right.

"I'm fine, thank you," the poor man said.

"Why aren't you working?" the rich man asked.

"Because I have harvested everything I need," said the poor man.

"But you have much more to harvest," said the rich man. "Pick more and sell it, and then you will begin to earn money. You can invest more money and buy a bigger farm, and then you will earn even more."

"And what will I do with all of that money?" the poor man asked.

"Well, then you can rest peacefully when you are old," the rich man said.

"But I was already resting peacefully when you found me," the poor man wisely said.

Christians have a secret, at least the successful ones do. It is the key to their commitment and to their abiding strength. It is how they can claim to be able to do all things through Christ. The secret is contentment. It has nothing to do with settling, and everything to do with attitude. Christians are content with Jesus Christ. They have a deep sense of satisfaction in who He is and what He has provided for them. This contentment is earned through practice and reinforced supernaturally by the Holy Spirit. Paul said he'd had much and he'd had little. Through these circumstances he had *learned* to be content.

Everything is possible through Christ. Whether God has blessed us with a lot or a little, we can learn to be content as well.

Philippians 4:10-23

DAY ONE

Word Study
PAUL'S PEACE

The Greek word for "content" used by Paul is a compound word made up of the words for "self" and "to suffice or have enough." In a purely dictionary sense, it means self-sufficient. But Paul did not use it in the sense of being proudly independent of anyone's help—even God's. He simply meant that, even if no other person supported him, he would still be at peace because of his faith in God. He was self-sufficient in that he trusted God to meet his needs.

PEACE AND CONTENTMENT (PHILIPPIANS 4:10–12)

Last week we spoke about peace and contentment. This week we'll look at how peace and contentment help make everything possible through our Lord Jesus. There is an amazing, mysterious power in what Jesus has given us as believers, but we need to grow into it. Just as you wouldn't give a toddler access to a nuclear reactor, God doesn't let us move into the realm of making the impossible possible until we master the basics. One of these building blocks of growth is achieving peace and contentment. Temptation is almost powerless when you are content. Even though the Philippian church has to expect suffering, they are to continue in good works with an attitude of peace and contentment. Between the lines, great power is revealed to the Philippian church.

CARE AND CONCERN

I rejoice greatly in the Lord that at last you have renewed your concern for me. Indeed, you have been concerned, but you had no opportunity to show it. I am not saying this because I am in need, for I have learned to be content whatever the circumstances. (Philippians 4:10–11)

It has long been known Asian cultures do a much better job than Western cultures of caring for their elderly. Although Asian cultures are becoming more Westernized, traditional expectations of caring for the elderly are still typical. In Asia the elderly are typically revered for their wisdom; the opportunity to sit and learn from a wise, older person is considered a privilege.

This concept is called *filial piety*.

The West claims to balance individual freedoms with filial piety, however, we don't always do as well as we should. In fact, much of the world does a better job, including Africa and the Middle East. Traditional Hebrew custom is to take care of the elderly, too, though it is preferred that parents have provided enough for themselves and even their grandchildren by the time they are old (Proverbs 13:22).

This is why Paul rejoices greatly at the Philippians' demonstration of support for him while he is in prison. Any parent will tell you one of life's most heartwarming moments is when your toddler hears a loud noise, leaves his toys, and runs over to make sure you are okay. In this way, Paul is rejoicing because his spiritual children are concerned for him. But he goes on to carefully explain why he rejoices. It is not because he needs care as the spiritual parent, but because members of the Philippian church's hearts are full of compassion and mercy.

Paul was intelligent and led by the Spirit, so I don't believe these two concepts are tied together coincidentally. Compassion, care, and respect for one's leaders and elders are further secrets to producing peace and contentment.

 What is your attitude toward your church's leaders? Do you pray for them as much as you mentally or verbally critique their leadership?

_____

_____

_____

 How could focusing on others impact your ability to overcome personal issues? (Philippians 2:4)

_____

_____

_____

CONTENTMENT

I know what it is to be in need, and I know what it is to have plenty. I have learned the secret of being content in any and every situation, whether well fed or hungry, whether living in plenty or in want. (Philippians 4:12)

Leadership teacher and popular author Kevin Eikenberry says, "It is easy to feel rich any time. Just count all the things you have that money can't buy."[18] I love this quote. It places in perspective things like good health and having a friend who loves you and who will listen to you. Half the world lives on less than two dollars a day, which makes most of us wealthy by comparison.

But these riches pale in comparison to the spiritual riches we have when we follow Christ. In fact, the Bible tells us clearly that wisdom, which is largely the reverence of God, is worth far more than gold and silver (Proverbs 3:14–18.) How can that be? Well, when you realize what a relationship with Jesus is worth, your desires begin to long for what is truly valuable and are a mere product of that relationship. Good health, peace, the diligence to make a good living—putting your relationship with Christ first will produce these things. This is what Paul understood. He was not focused on amassing wealth, yet he found contentment. In Paul's early life he excelled far above his peers and was undoubtedly on track to becoming the High Priest—one of the most powerful political seats in Israel. Yet he had no peace. As we saw last week, he counted his striving all as loss compared to gaining and serving Christ. The difference is that Paul realized he now had a much-needed Savior. He had no pressure to live up to outside expectations; he simply had to be obedient to his Savior. He had no need for security because his Savior had already promised to provide it for him. He had no need for treasure because he understood and believed he was amassing wealth in eternity.

> **"There is nothing holier, or better, or safer, than to content ourselves with the authority of Christ alone."**
>
> **John Calvin**

> **"Contentment with what we have is absolutely vital to our spiritual health."**
>
> **Jerry Bridges**

 **Doctrine**
MONEY

One of the most frequently misquoted verses in the Bible is 1 Timothy 6:10: *"For the love of money is a root of all kinds of evil. . . ."* Money is not the root of all kinds of evil, but the love of money is. Insecurity or discontentment is not based on the presence or absence of money, but on how much we love or desire money.

Paul had learned the secret. The Gnostics, who were teaching heresy at the time, claimed to possess "secret knowledge," and this led them to believe it was okay to do ungodly things. They thought knowledge was higher than anything physical, so they could practice any number of sinful behaviors, because their secret knowledge saved them. Paul is saying he also has secret knowledge. But his secret knowledge is contentment. Contentment allows him peace in times when others would panic. Instead of allowing him to sin, contentment keeps him close to Christ.

Paul understood the secret to peace and contentment was to serve the Lord and serve others. In this way, all things become possible because it's up to God to accomplish His plan. You're just submitting to it.

How important is security to your peace, especially in light of recent economic events? How practical is it to focus on material security (Matthew 6:25–32)?

_____

_____

_____

_____

APPLY Do you truly believe there is security in Christ? If so, how does He make you secure?

_____

_____

_____

_____

Responding to Scripture

How would you describe the big idea of Philippians 4:10–12?

_____

_____

_____

_____

Responding to Life

In what way could you most readily apply the main lesson from this passage to your life?

_____

_____

_____

_____

_____

Dear heavenly Father, thank You for providing for me in every way through Your Son Jesus. Where I struggle to trust You, please fill me with peace and contentment; remind me I already live with You in eternity. Please help me to focus on others, especially my leaders and elders, in helping them do the work of the Great Commission. I pray You will help me to focus on the eternal rewards of serving others, and in this way help me to achieve what I thought impossible. In Jesus name I pray. Amen.

POWER IN CHRIST (PHILIPPIANS 4:13)

Philippians 4:10-23

DAY TWO

Thousands of years ago, God created Adam and Eve in the garden of Eden. Life was exactly as God intended it, with only love, joy, and the absence of death. In this utopia, Adam and Eve thrived in the garden with no struggles and no cares. The best part was God would walk with them in the garden and spend time with them. God's presence sustained them in their carefree existence.

As we know, Adam and Eve were unaware they had a mortal enemy in the garden. Satan craftily planted doubt in their minds—doubt that God had their best intentions at heart; doubt that He would provide everything they needed. They sinned, and life became a disaster compared to what they had known before. Adam now had to work in his own strength. The ground couldn't produce as easily as it had, because his sin had brought a curse, even to the ground. Eve would now experience terrible pain in childbirth.

Life was surely difficult. They could no longer walk with God for they were ashamed, full of guilt, and wanted to hide. But God had a plan. It would not be easy, and the sacrifice was nothing short of astounding. He planned to send His only begotten Son to redeem them. Through Jesus Christ, the impossible again became possible.

CLOTHE YOURSELF WITH CHRIST

I can do everything through him who gives me strength. (Philippians 4:13)

I've heard many people quote this Scripture—athletes, political candidates, even soldiers. Does Paul really mean he is like Superman, and he can do anything he wants through Christ who will make it happen for him? Young's Literal Translation says, *"For all things I have strength, in Christ's strengthening me."* Paul is saying that through reliance on Christ, anything God allows Paul to go through, or anything God has called him to accomplish, is sufficiently provided for in Jesus. Notice, however, Paul has to rely on Jesus and continue to be transformed into His image to get these results.

Jesus will only give us strength to accomplish God's will. When He gives you strength, however, all things within God's will for you become possible.

> *"In themselves, believers have no life, or strength, or spiritual power. All that they have of vital religion comes from Christ. They are what they are, and feel what they feel, and do what they do, because they draw out of Jesus a continual supply of grace, help and ability."*
>
> **J. C. Ryle**

It seems too good to be true. But this is how Paul lived. It is how those who have graduated to heaven live—by the power of God. Even Jesus said, "By myself I can do nothing …" (John 5:30).

By reading the Gospels, we can learn how to become more like Jesus. By studying Him, we can emulate Him. Then we allow His Holy Spirit within us to work through us, making all things possible. In fact, this reliance protects us as well. God wants us to be completely covered by Jesus as a shield covers a soldier.

Consider the following Scripture:

> *Rather, clothe yourselves with the Lord Jesus Christ, and do not think about how to gratify the desires of the sinful nature. (Romans 13:14)*

📖 Think about the function of clothing. What implications does clothing yourself with Christ have for you (Galatians 3:27)?

_____

_____

_____

APPLY Consider the challenges you face today and how Jesus would approach them. If you are clothed with Christ, how should you approach them?

_____

_____

_____

_____

Word Study

EMPOWERMENT

The word for "strength" in Philippians 4:13 is *dunamo*, the word upon which the English word "dynamite" is based. It could be translated "empower." What we get from Christ is not some abstract power. It is His strength empowering us, a force within that enables us to do what we otherwise could not. We don't go and get Christ's power. Christ comes and empowers us.

SOMEONE TO LEAN ON

> *I can do everything through him who gives me strength. (Philippians 4:13)*

In 1980 the American Psychiatric Association added "Reactive Attachment Disorder" to the Diagnostic and Statistical Manual of Mental Disorders. RAD is a condition in which a child displays disturbingly inappropriate ways of relating socially. This can be manifested as either angry or highly inappropriate ways of social interaction such as verbal bullying, disrespect, etc., or an excessive familiarity with strangers. RAD occurs when a child is severely neglected and is shown little affection in infancy and during the toddler years. It severely affects a child in youth and throughout adulthood. It is one of the saddest things to think about, but with the prevalence of drug addiction and poverty, an increasing number of children suffer from this disorder. What a sad testament to why loving relationships between a parent and child are so crucial. They can determine who we become.

Numerous studies have shown that even pets improve the quality of one's life. It has been proven that having a pet reduces stress, lowers blood pressure more than drugs, and even encourages exercise. What am I trying to say? Just this: relationships, even with animals, which can't talk back, enable us to live better lives. It is how we were created.

Relationship is also the key to how we can draw strength from Christ. Just as we talk with friends and learn to trust them, we talk with Jesus and learn the same. Even better, we learn He is an utterly reliable friend and loves us more than we can imagine. The supernatural part is that while our friendship with Him is growing deeper, we are growing stronger. We are increasing in wisdom and growing in character. Our relationship with Him determines who we become.

The closer our relationship with Jesus becomes, the greater the benefit to God's kingdom and our lives. Throughout the Old and New Testaments, God uses marriage imagery–the deepest form of *voluntary* relationship–to describe His relationship with His beloved church. That's us! Even going all the way back to the beginning, it would appear God was creating the church for Himself, just as He created Eve for Adam. That is how important our relationship with Him is and how much He loves us.

Scripture also tells us believers are heirs with Christ (Romans 8:17). If we are heirs, it means we have an inheritance, a claim, to the fortunes of heaven. Let that sink in for a second. You are rich! Now if we are heirs and the bride of Christ, what else does that mean for us? Heirs are those deemed by a father worthy to receive all that he has acquired in life. That is who we are to God. All He has is ours. A bride is the one for whom a groom waits, the one he loves and wants to be with forever. God, the Creator of heaven and earth, is waiting for the church to become his perfect bride. Again our relationship with Him determines who we become. This theme repeats itself throughout Scripture. Our strength, our ability to do all things, is determined by our relationship with Christ.

Even when our closest loved ones on earth fail us, as everyone will, Jesus is the ultimate "significant other." He said He will never leave us nor forsake us (Hebrews 13:5). He loves us dearly, but that is not all. He actually paved the way for all things to become possible for us. He defeated sin, defeated death, and has sealed the deal with His Spirit in us. When you get a revelation of what is available to you through the work Jesus did, it will completely revolutionize your life. If you haven't had such an experience, pray that God will restore the joy of your salvation so you will find strength in the realization of what Jesus has done for you (Psalm 51:12) and of His love for you.

APPLY What if you achieved your greatest dream tomorrow? What would be next for you? What do you believe the greatest achievement in life could be (Philippians 3:12-14)?

_____

_____

_____

_____

Do you think Jesus complains when you need help from Him? What might His reaction be? How might you draw more strength from Him (Hebrews 4:15–16)?

_____

_____

_____

> *"It was well worth standing a while in the fire, for such an opportunity of experiencing and exhibiting the power and faithfulness of God's promises."*
>
> **John Newton**

_____
_____

Responding to Scripture

Write out the central idea of Philippians 4:13 in your own words.

_____
_____
_____

Responding to Life

Where could you apply this teaching most readily in your life right now?

_____
_____
_____
_____

Responding to God

 Dear heavenly Father, thank You for giving me all the strength I need in the relationship I have with Your Son Jesus. Please help me to understand more deeply what is available for me from the treasures of your kingdom and, more importantly, how to appropriate them. Lord Jesus, You know my shortcomings, but I am grateful You pick me up and dust me off and then show me how to walk like You did on earth. Please work through me in a greater way and use Your strength in my life to do your will. I love You Lord. In Your name I pray. Amen.

Philippians 4:10–23

DAY THREE

PROVISIONS THAT ARE PLEASING (PHILIPPIANS 4:14–20)

One of the most faith-building aspects of my relationship with God has been receiving His provisions in miraculous ways. Personally, I am still in awe as I look back at how God provided for our family, whether it was financially, or providing godly spouses for our children, or providing opportunities to bring some of the most unlikely friends to Christ. God provides when you least expect it. But God also calls on us to be providers.

When God took on a human body and taught us the principles of heaven in the person of Jesus, He reduced the entire Mosaic Law down to two commandments: "Love your God with all your heart, soul, mind and strength," and "Love your neighbor as yourself." God obviously takes consideration for our fellow man seriously. Have you ever wondered why?

In Matthew 25:31–46, Jesus draws a clear line between the righteous and the ungodly. Where that line is drawn, however, may surprise some of us. If you read that Scripture, you'll see Jesus said if you feed, clothe, or take care of even a beggar, it is the same as doing it for Jesus Himself. In the same way, those who neglect actual works of righteousness but claim to be followers of Christ need to think long and hard about how deep their relationship with Him really goes.

PARTNERING IN THE GOSPEL

Yet it was good of you to share in my troubles. Moreover, as you Philippians know, in the early days of your acquaintance with the gospel, when I set out from Macedonia, not one church shared with me in the matter of giving and receiving, except you only; for even when I was in Thessalonica, you sent me aid again and again when I was in need. (Philippians 4:14–16)

In hindsight, because we see the big picture of Paul's ministry, it's easy to think of him as a celebrity. We might picture him traveling on the finest cruise liners, demanding a beachfront room and a healthy honorarium before he'd even look at the speaking invitation.

In reality, Paul says the Philippians were the only church who partnered with him. At times he worked for a living on the mission field (Acts 18:3) and usually lived with believing families. Anyone who has traveled in ministry knows how difficult that can be. Yet Paul's only focus was to go into a city's synagogue, preach Christ, and build a church with those who believed.

Paul says something interesting in the first verse: *"Yet it was good of you to share in my troubles."* The Philippians were partners with Paul. Ponder that for a moment. Whatever great wealth Paul has in heaven, the Philippian church has a matching portion of that wealth because they partnered with him in his ministry.

We occasionally hear of ministries that abuse partnership. Sadly, there are some in "ministry" who just love money. But there are those like Paul, ministries that are honest and simply have a desire to spread the Gospel. When you provide for these ministries, you are God's hands in that situation, and he will greatly reward you. That doesn't mean God is going to return your money with interest over time; that is not the focus of our giving. If you support ministries that are doing great work and bearing real fruit, you are a partner in winning the souls that are saved through them.

 If you support a ministry, in what ways might God reward you? (2 Corinthians 9:6)

_____

_____

_____

If you were called into ministry, how might you approach fundraising? How do you respond when asked by those in ministry who are raising support? Do you have a strategy for determining which ministries will receive financial support from you and which will not?

_____

_____

Put Yourself in Their Shoes
RELATIONSHIP AND GIVING

It is important to remember Paul founded the church in Philippi and the relationships he had with its members likely inspired their generosity. On the other hand, the Macedonian churches gave sacrificially and beyond their ability to give to Christians they did not even know and would never meet: the struggling church in Jerusalem (2 Corinthians 8:1ff.) Relationships may or may not play a role in giving. The leading of the Holy Spirit is the most important factor.

Doctrine
TREASURES IN HEAVEN

Jesus made a strong point about treasures in heaven versus treasures on earth. When we invest the money God has given us in kingdom work, we are laying up treasure (rewards) in heaven. Jesus put it plainly: *"You cannot serve both God and Money"* (Matthew 6:19–24).

Doctrine
THE MEETING OF NEEDS

Philippians 4:19 is a verse that is quoted often without regard to its context—the promise that God will meet all one's needs through the riches of Christ. It is important to note that Paul wrote those words to a group of Christians who had sacrificed in order to give to another who was in need (Paul). The point is that as we sacrifice to meet the needs of others, God in turn will meet our needs (2 Corinthians 9:6–8).

_____

_____

_____

> "Our heavenly Father never takes anything from his children unless he means to give them something better."
>
> George Müller

> "If God gave you ten times as much as you give him, could you live on it?"
>
> Anonymous

REAL SECURITY

Not that I am looking for a gift, but I am looking for what may be credited to your account. I have received full payment and even more; I am amply supplied, now that I have received from Epaphroditus the gifts you sent. They are a fragrant offering, an acceptable sacrifice, pleasing to God. And my God will meet all your needs according to his glorious riches in Christ Jesus. To our God and Father be glory for ever and ever. Amen. (Philippians 4:17–20)

In Oxford, England, there is a school for youths aged four- to thirteen-years- old called the Dragon School. This institution has two fascinating programs. One, called "Big Give," gathers information from about seven thousand international charities. The other is called "Philanthropy in Schools." In these programs, students are provided the resources to research a great number of charities and decide which one should receive a donation from them. The money comes from their parents or their own savings, but the highlight of the program is a competition in which students identify a charity they love and create a presentation to raise money for it. Many students who have been through the program say it has changed their lives.

While these young people are certainly learning how to research a worthy charity, they are also learning something much greater: how to give. Philanthropy is deeply rewarding. In our Scripture passage above, while Paul praises the Philippians, he goes on to specify the main reason for his praise: "Not that I am looking for a gift, but I am looking for what may be credited to your account." Paul knew God would provide for him one way or another. He must have heard Peter explain how Jesus told him to pull a coin out of a fish's mouth for taxes. He heard about Jesus feeding the five thousand. Paul was praising the Philippians because they got it. They understood, whether out of pure love and obedience or because they knew a good cause when they saw it, that God is well pleased when we give.

It may sound strange, but the act of giving benefits the giver as much as the receiver. When we give to others, we become more like Christ. We depend on God for our own provisions while being obedient to provide for those He puts in our path who cannot provide for themselves.

When you allow God to provide for others *through* you, you allow God to provide *for* you. Paul understood this and praised the Philippians because he knew God could bless them even more. They could be trusted as conduits to further God's work.

In God's eyes, whether you provide a homeless person a meal or a plane ticket for a missionary, you build the greatest security for yourself that you ever could imagine.

📖 When you give, is it purposeful or on a whim? How might purposeful giving yield greater rewards for the kingdom and for you? (2 Corinthians 9:10–14; Isaiah 32:8)

_____

_____
_____
_____

 APPLY Has God ever miraculously provided for you? Would you share how?

_____
_____
_____

Doctrine
DOXOLOGY

Paul's final words in this section—Philippians 4:20—are a doxology: an expression of praise to God. Paul's longest and most well-known doxology is found in Romans 11:33–36. His motivation in Romans was the mercy of God, while his motivation in Philippians was the gracious generosity of God through and to His people.

Responding to Scripture

How would you summarize Paul's main emphasis in Philippians 4:14–20?

_____
_____
_____
_____

Responding to Life

What would be the most immediate application you could make to your life from this passage?

_____
_____
_____
_____

Responding to God

Dear heavenly Father, thank You for providing for me. The greatest gift You have given me is salvation, which I want to share with all those who have not received it. Please help me to understand how to best give to Your kingdom with my time, talent, and treasure. Please show me how, as I give, You are able to provide for me in ways I may not even realize or expect. I pray Your will is done on earth, and I want to be a part of seeing that happen. In Jesus holy name I pray. Amen.

PARTING GRACE AND GREETINGS (PHILIPPIANS 4:21-23)

One of our family's favorite television shows was *Extreme Makeover; Home Edition*. The show was about a group of volunteers—contractors, designers, decorators, plumbers, etc.—who all came together to give of their time to renovate or recreate a new home for poor, underprivileged families. What struck me every time I watched the show was the amazing accomplishment that resulted when people worked together, while at the same time using their individual gifts.

In 1 Corinthians 12, Paul gives a wonderful illustration of how a body has many parts with many functions, but all work together for the single good of the person. The body in Paul's analogy is clearly the Body of Christ. We are Christ's body in the world—his hands, his feet, his heart. It is interesting to consider that everything is possible through Christ when viewed from this perspective.

STRENGTH IN UNITY

Greet all the saints in Christ Jesus. The brothers who are with me send greetings. All the saints send you greetings, especially those who belong to Caesar's household. (Philippians 4:21–22)

No one can argue that Paul's letters are filled with deep, godly wisdom and multiple layers of truth crammed into every verse. Paul had such a great knowledge of Scripture that when he was filled with the Holy Spirit, he received such astounding revelations that Satan's harassment of him was relentless. God allowed it so Paul wouldn't become conceited (2 Corinthians 12:7–10.)

It shouldn't be surprising that every line and word Paul places in his letters have meaning. Even in something as simple as a greeting, Paul subtly continues to reinforce his theme. Paul repeatedly preaches strength through faith in Christ and consistently teaches about the immense possibilities when a believer trusts God. Paul also speaks consistently about the church being the Body of Christ, and in fact, what he calls the "burden of the churches" weighs on him heavily (2 Corinthians 11:28 NLT).

When Paul takes the trouble to write greetings to and from believers to one another, he sets an example. Like a true father, Paul shows instead of tells the churches what a major source of strength is. If they are the Body of Christ, and they can do all things through Christ who strengthens them, surely unity is critical in their development and accomplishments. In every letter, Paul ends with these greetings. They build closeness and a sense of solidarity among the churches in various cities.

Today our churches probably compete more than they cooperate, but Paul reveals a great source of strength in unity in his communication with churches. I believe he does this deliberately and is intentional in the way he does it too. I enjoy reading the ending of Paul's letters, because they give us a little inside glimpse of the families of believers who paved the way for us.

I wonder if Paul knew his letters would last beyond his lifetime, for he is showing us that what was accomplished wasn't done by him alone. In the same way, we also should find great strength in unity as believers

> *Carry each other's burdens, and in this way you will fulfill the law of Christ. (Galatians 6:2)*

APPLY Does your closest friendship revolve around Jesus? If not, what reward does that friendship revolve around?

_____

_____

_____

_____

APPLY What do you see as your role in the Body of Christ? What gift(s) has God given you (1 Corinthians 12:7–11)?

_____

_____

_____

_____

STRENGTH THROUGH GRACE

> *The grace of the Lord Jesus Christ be with your spirit. Amen. (Philippians 4:23)*

How many times have you heard we are saved by faith? Did you know this statement is actually incorrect? Faith has a major part to play in appropriating, or claiming our salvation, but the true saving factor is God's grace:

> *For it is by grace you have been saved, through faith—and this not from yourselves, it is the gift of God. (Ephesians 2:8)*

So grace saves us through faith. That makes sense. But let me ask you another question. We also know Jesus said He'd never leave us nor forsake us (Hebrews 13:5–6). So why is it that Paul finds it necessary to pray the grace of Jesus be with the Philippians? It's a thought-provoking question, but the answer is quite simple. Humans, even Christians, are stubborn and tend to resist the grace of God rather than inviting it to do its transforming work.

Grace is a powerful force, and it does not stop once we are saved (see Titus 2:11–14). Grace is at work before we are saved, while we are being saved, and throughout the process of our sanctification. Grace will not stop until we are conformed to the image of Jesus Christ, but we are called to cooperate with this process. Paul accomplished the things he did for the kingdom of God precisely because he submitted to the empowering and ongoing work of grace in his life.

The difference is the awareness of grace as a strengthening force. Grace has been explained as unmerited favor or as the acronym "God's Riches At Christ's Expense." Both of these are accurate. However, they don't tell the full story of grace. Though God's grace is not an excuse to tolerate sin, God has provided forgiveness for every sin you will ever commit by His powerful grace. That same grace will teach us to say no to sin and to live a godly life!

"A person who says he believes in God but never goes to church is like one who says he believes in education but never goes to school."

Franklin Clark Fry

Doctrine
GRACE

One of the ways God manifests grace in the church is through spiritual gifts. Paul writes in Romans 12:3-8 that God has given a "measure" of grace to each believer and that we are to serve the church by means of that grace. Spiritual gifts—the manifestation of God's grace—are mentioned in four chapters of the New Testament: Romans 12, 1 Corinthians 12, Ephesians 4, and 1 Peter 4. None of the lists of gifts is complete—the gifts mentioned are representative of how Christ works in and through His body. Every Christian should know what his or her spiritual gift is.

> *When God forgives he forgets. He buries our sins in the sea and puts up a sign on the bank saying, "No fishing allowed."*
>
> **Corrie ten Boom**

This means you can forget the past. Forget the mistake you made five minutes ago and look forward, because God is ready to forgive you and empower you to achieve your wildest dreams in Him. This is why Paul so often greets and centers his good-byes around grace. Praise God!

APPLY Do you feel you have been given grace by God to accomplish His will in your life? Are you serving Him in that area (Romans 12:3–6a)?

_____

_____

_____

_____

_____

APPLY Do you find it difficult to believe God has forgotten your past and sees you in your complete potential? What practices can you adopt that could help you grow in seeing yourself through His eyes?

_____

_____

_____

_____

_____

_____

_____

Read Titus 2:11–14. How do you think God's grace teaches us?

_____

_____

_____

_____

_____

Responding to Scripture

What is Paul's big idea in the final verses of our study (Philippians 4:21–23)?

_____

_____

_____

Responding to Life

How might you apply the content of these verses to your life beginning today?

_____

_____

_____

_____

_____

_____

Responding to God

 Dear heavenly Father, I love You so much. Thank You for my church body, who are genuinely concerned about my well-being and spiritual growth. I pray You will help me develop relationships within the church that are deeper than any other friendships. I know my Christian brothers and sisters are born of the light, and I will know them forever. Please help me to be a source of Christ's strength to them, and in the process, help me to grow stronger in Your grace. I love You, Lord, and I want to show it by loving Your church. In Jesus wonderful name I pray. Amen.

REVIEW FOR FOLLOWING GOD

The fact that anything is possible to us spiritually seems more like fanciful rhetoric than reality. Like many spiritual truths, it takes a fair amount of application before the revelations and realizations are illuminated. The amazing truth, however, is everything is truly provided for us. Everything our heart—not our flesh—desires is really possible through Christ.

I believe the trouble we have in receiving this truth is doubt of our intrinsic value to God. If you are a parent, think about how much your children mean to you. Even though they don't always behave as you wish, do they ever lose value to you? Would you ever stop doing anything you could to help them? Of course not. Why should God be any different?

God greatly desires to see you succeed, and He has provided everything you need to do so. In this week's studies, you should begin to see a clear pathway to greater possibilities in your life.

REVIEW OF DAY 1: PEACE AND CONTENTMENT (PHILIPPIANS 4:10–12)

In modern society, people are desperate for peace. With everything from rumors of wars increasing, to severe natural disasters climbing at an astonishing rate, to overpopulation and overcrowding, the world looks as though it's starting to lose peace and contentment. But we shouldn't be affected by these things.

First, Jesus warned us things would get bad before He returned, and He told us not to worry (Matthew 24:6). Secondly, while all this craziness is escalating, we have the remedy right in front of us. We simply need to care for one another as family and put our service to the Lord first. In these ways, we have peace and security from our spiritual community and freedom from artificial pressures. It is His responsibility to guide and provide for us, and He most certainly will.

Philippians 4:10-23

DAY FIVE

**Put Yourself in Their Shoes**
PROVISION

Paul's contentment was not because he believed "the church" owed him a living. Indeed, Paul worked as a tentmaker when he needed income (Acts 18:3) and did not ask for or expect support from the churches. He maintained his independence in that way so as not to suggest that he was in the ministry for financial gain. Part of his trust in God's provision was his own God-given ability to work.

Doctrine
EVERYTHING

In Philippians 4:13, Paul doesn't say he can do "anything" through Christ. Rather, "everything" refers to that which God expects of Him that might be a challenge to the natural man spiritually or emotionally. Everything that was God's will for Paul he knew he could do through Christ.

"Everything we have comes from God. When we give to Him or others it is because He has first given to us."

1 Chronicles 29:14

APPLY How peaceful and content are you? Do you believe where you are, is God's best for you?

_____

_____

_____

_____

REVIEW OF DAY 2: POWER IN CHRIST (PHILIPPIANS 4:13)

These days if we say someone is co-dependent, it usually means that person is disproportionately reliant on another person in a relationship. It usually carries a negative connotation, since our culture values independence and individuality so dearly, and, to a certain degree, I think it is negative in that context. When two fallible people come together in a relationship, and if one is emotionally helpless in many areas and shows no signs of growth, the relationship is typically destined for problems.

We are all fallible, but Christ is infinitely strong and able to carry us through anything and everything. In fact, it only makes sense for us to be dependent on Him. He wants our dependence, and our heavenly Father has specifically provided for us in the person of Christ. This is done through relationship, which is so valuable and essential to us. Without a relationship with Him, we are like orphans traumatized daily by this world. But Christ's loving, caring arms can heal a lifetime of wounds. He is our power, and we should rely on Him for everything.

APPLY Do you think your ideas of independence and individuality affect your ability to rely on God? How could you change that?

_____

_____

_____

_____

REVIEW OF DAY 3: PROVISIONS THAT ARE PLEASING (PHILIPPIANS 4:14-20)

In recent years, the stock market has shown everyone just how volatile this world can be. Due to corruption in the housing industry, an artificial bubble–value–was created, and before long, it imploded. This event is a perfect example of the difference between temporary investments grounded in a sinful world and the eternal investments grounded in the kingdom of God.

There are many ministries in the same period (in contrast to the stock market) that saw an increase in their donations and ministry. More souls were saved, more people were healed, and more families were saved from the destruction of divorce. The list goes on. Especially in times of trouble, people wise up and tend to seek God again. This is how it was all through the Old Testament, and this is how it is now.

The secular media, however, won't report on the growth of the church in these times. But I assure you it's happening. One similarity with the stock market, however, is dividends of productive ministries will be reaped by those investing in them as well. But for reasons beyond this, it is our duty to be God's provision for these ministries. Indeed, didn't we receive salvation as a result of someone's ministry effort?

APPLY Do you see giving as a requirement or an opportunity? Explain.

_____

_____

_____

_____

_____

REVIEW OF DAY 4: PARTING GRACE AND GREETINGS (PHILIPPIANS 4:21–23)

In something as simple as a farewell greeting, Paul manages to bond the church together as family. It is quite likely, Paul's family disapproved of him, as his father was a prominent and wealthy Pharisee (Acts 23:6.) We don't know whether his own family later converted to Christ. Perhaps for this reason, Paul values and cherishes his Christian family and encourages them to bond at every opportunity.

Many of us place our families and childhood, secular friendships before our Christian ones. But that is not what Jesus wants us to do. He tells us:

> *If anyone comes to me and does not hate his father and mother, his wife and children, his brothers and sisters—yes, even his own life—he cannot be my disciple.—Luke 14:26*

Jesus doesn't mean we have to literally hate our family and friends in order to be His disciple. Instead, he means comparatively. We should always consider Christ first, even before our families, a difficult thing to do. But as we struggle with learning how this will work out in our lives, we can ask Him for the grace to do it, and He will grant it. I believe that goes for His church too. With Christ as our central focus, we should love each other as we love Jesus (Matthew 25:40). We are to love each other so much that the world sees and is led to inquire about how it is possible that a group of people could love each other so much. But we must be careful not to mistake church work for Christ's work and get so caught up in activities that we are not tending to the stewardship God has given us for our own families.

APPLY Can you cite examples in your life of loving Christ more than your biological family? Think about how your love for Christ ought to be recognizable as a priority in your life.

_____

_____

_____

_____

_____

_____

_____

_____

REVIEW PHILIPPIANS 4:10-23

Review the Scriptures and content of this week's lessons and identify three ideas, themes, or action points that struck you from what you studied this week. Especially look for ideas to apply to your own life.

1. _____
_____
_____
_____
_____

2. _____
_____
_____
_____
_____

3. _____
_____
_____
_____

REFLECT ON GALATIANS 6:2

Carry each other's burdens, and in this way you will fulfill the law of Christ.

In this cross-reference Scripture, how do you think God primarily provides for His church?

_____
_____
_____
_____

APPLY How can you put this into practice in your own life?

_____
_____
_____
_____
_____
_____
_____
_____

Heavenly Father, I thank You for this week's study on everything being possible through Jesus. Thank You for everything You've done in my life thus far and for helping me to accomplish all I have. Even though I may see myself as small, help me to see myself as a spiritual giant because of Your presence in me. Please show me I am capable of doing anything for Your kingdom. Please help me understand how much of Your strength is available through Your church and help me to be that strength to others as well. In Jesus powerful name I pray. Amen.

Summary

My friend, what a wonderful journey this has been! I feel as though we have sat in a Roman jail, traveled the dusty streets of Macedonia, and sailed across the Mediterranean with the Apostle Paul. We listened to him preach in the streets, counsel with fellow disciples, and share his heart in a letter written not only to the believers of Philippi, but to each of us today.

First Peter 3:15 tells us, to "Always be prepared to give an answer to everyone who asks you to give the reason for the hope that you have. But do this with gentleness and respect...." Therefore, imagine you are talking to a new believer in Christ and he or she asks you what Paul meant when he wrote, "... to live is Christ" (Philippians 1:21).

Review the last page of Day 5 from each of the eight lessons and make some notes concerning the focus from each week. Then, in your own words, write out a brief letter (see next page) to your friend, explaining what you believe Paul meant by his words, "...to live is Christ," and how your friend can experience the life of Christ on a daily basis.

Dear Friend,

Here is what I believe Paul meant when he wrote, ". . . to live is Christ.:"

_____
_____
_____
_____
_____
_____
_____
_____
_____
_____
_____
_____
_____
_____
_____
_____
_____
_____
_____
_____
_____
_____
_____
_____
_____
_____
_____

Bibliography

1. Tan, P.L. *Encyclopedia 7700 Illustrations: Signs of the Times*. Garland, TX: [Communications, Ind.], 1996.

2. Ibid.

3. McGee, Vernon. *The Epistles Philippians and Colossians*. Nashville, TN: Thomas Nelson (1991). *p* 16.

4. McGuirk, Nancy. *Rest Assured: Devotions for Souls in a Restless World*. Nashville, TN: B&H Publishing Group (2007). *p.* 58.

5. Tan, P.L. *Encyclopedia 7700 Illustrations*

6. McGuirk, Nancy. *Rest Assured,* p. 120.

7. http://robert.williamsonline.us/2005/07/john-piper-on-legalism

8. Tan, P.L. *Encyclopedia 7700 Illustrations*.

9. Willard, Dallas. *Divine Conspiracy.* San Francisco: Harper (1998).

10. Chambers. Oswald. *My Utmost for His Highest.* Grand Rapids, MI: Discovery House Publishers (1992, 1935).

11. Tan, P.L. *Encyclopedia 7700 Illustrations*.

12. Ibid.

13. Wiersbe, Warren. *Be Joyful*. Colorado Springs, CO: Chariot Victor Publishing, Cook Communications (1974).

14. Ibid.

15. Tan, P.L. *Encyclopedia 7700 Illustrations*.

16. Ortberg, Pederson, Poling. *Growth: Training vs. Trying (Pursuing Spiritual Transformation)*. Grand Rapids, MI: Zondervan (October 1, 2002). *p.* 16.

17. http://www.aerospaceweb.org/question/nature/q0237.shtml

18. Eikenberry, Kevin: *Remarkable Leadership: Unleashing Your Inner Potential One Skill At A Time*. San Francisco: Jossey Bass (2007).

Finding Your Way to God

*Jesus answered, "I am the way and the truth and the life.
No one comes to the Father except through me."*
John 14:6

Two distinct feelings can surface when we are lost. First is the feeling of hopelessness that comes when you don't have a clue which way to turn. Who hasn't felt that way in an unfamiliar city or neighborhood? You know your destination is reachable, but you know you'll never make it without help.

The second feeling is frustration. You ask someone for help, follow their directions, and after many twists and turns realize they gave you misleading information. You trusted their guidance, but with a frustrating result: you were still lost.

There are many people today who feel both hopeless and frustrated in their search for God. Not only do they not know how to find Him on their own, they're overwhelmed by the directions they've been given (many of which seem to point in opposite directions).

Spiritual hopelessness and frustration are symptoms of being lost, and it is just as possible to be lost spiritually as it is to be lost geographically. To find our way spiritually we need to turn to the directions that have helped millions of people reach their destination for many centuries: the Bible. God caused the Bible to be written to preserve a permanent record of how to find Him and walk through life with Him.

Before looking at what the Bible says about finding God, here's an important truth to remember: we don't find God; He finds us. It's as if you traveled to an unfamiliar neighborhood to visit a friend, and the friend got worried when you didn't arrive and went out searching for you. You didn't find your friend; your friend found you. Jesus told a number of stories in Luke 15 that illustrate this truth. His words in Luke 19:10 say it best: "For the Son of Man came to seek and to save what was lost."

If you feel lost when it comes to knowing God—hopeless, frustrated, or otherwise—it's probably because God is looking for you. He sends His Holy Spirit into the world to awaken the hearts of people so they will come to see what He sees—that they are, in fact, lost (John 16:7–11). Without a knowledge of the bad news that we're lost, the good news that we can be found isn't nearly as valuable!

The Bible records an interesting conversation between Jesus and a Jewish leader who sensed he was lost. Nicodemus knew there was something unique and divine about Jesus, and he needed directions to the kingdom of heaven. Jesus told Nicodemus he could only get there by being born again—experiencing a spiritual birth just as he had once experienced a physical birth. Reading Nicodemus' story is a good illustration of one's man feeling of "lostness." Jesus' answers to him will serve as directions for you as well (John 3:1-16).

Here are four landmarks that every person seeking God will ultimately encounter:

1. GOD LOVES US AND DESIRES GOOD THINGS FOR US:

"For I know the plans I have for you," declares the LORD, "plans to prosper you and not to harm you, plans to give you hope and a future." (Jeremiah 29:11; see also John 10:10)

2. WE ARE LOST BECAUSE OF OUR SIN. IT KEEPS US SEPARATED FROM GOD.

For all have sinned and fall short of the glory of God. (Romans 3:23; see also Romans 6:23a)

3. GOD HAS PROVIDED A PATH FOR FORGIVENESS THROUGH JESUS CHRIST.

For God so loved the world that he gave his one and only Son, that whoever believes in him shall not perish but have eternal life. (John 3:16; see also Romans 5:8)

4. WE MUST RECEIVE THE FREE GIFTS OF FORGIVENESS AND ETERNAL LIFE OFFERED TO US THROUGH CHRIST.

. . . but the gift of God is eternal life in Christ Jesus our Lord. (Romans 6:23b; see also Ephesians 2:8–9)

How do we receive God's gifts of forgiveness and eternal life? We receive His gifts just as we would receive a gift from a good friend. We reach out for it . . . we embrace it . . . we say "thank you" . . . and we put it to use with gratitude.

In addition, there is one condition for receiving God's gifts: faith. Hebrews 11:6 says, "And without faith it is impossible to please God, because anyone who comes to Him must believe that He exists and that He rewards those who earnestly seek Him." We exercise faith in God by accepting Christ as Lord and

Savior of our life. John 1:12 says, "Yet to all who received Him, to those who believed in His name, He gave the right to become children of God."

How do we express our faith in God? Prayer is the simplest way. You can find God through accepting Christ by praying a prayer as simple as this:

"Dear God, Thank you for sending Jesus Christ to die and pay the penalty for my sins. I accept your gifts of forgiveness and eternal life by believing in Christ as my Lord and Savior. Please help me to live a life that is pleasing to you in every way. Amen."

If knowing God is the sincere desire of your heart, then He has heard and answered your prayer (1 John 5:14-15). And several things have happened:

- Christ now lives in you (Colossians 1:27)
- Your sins are forgiven (Colossians 1:14)
- You have become a child of God (John 1:12)
- You have received eternal life (John 5:24)
- And you have been born again as a new spiritual person and entered in a new life (John 3:3; 2 Corinthians 5:17; 1 Thessalonians 5:18; Hebrews 11:6)

CONTINUING YOUR JOURNEY WITH GOD

"So then, just as you received Christ Jesus as Lord, continue to live in Him" (Colossians 2:16)

By putting your trust in Jesus Christ as Savior and Lord, you have made the most important decision of your life. Not only have you been saved from the eternal consequences of your sins, you have also been given the gift of eternal life and membership in God's "forever family." And, here on earth, you have been given the gift of the Holy Spirit who has come to live within you to guide and comfort you in your Christian life. Through the Holy Spirit, Christ is alive in you each day (Galatians 2:20).

Your acceptance of Christ is not the end of your journey to faith—it is the beginning of your journey of faith! You will begin to look at life through faith-colored glasses, seeing the hand of God at work in and around you every day. Life will be a privilege and responsibility, a means for glorifying God as you learn to please Him in all things. And you will discover that what glorifies Him most is also best for you. Life becomes a win-win situation with Christ—God is glorified and you are loved, protected, and directed.

Just as your life before knowing Christ had characteristics, your new life with Christ will take on characteristics as well. Prayer, Bible study, worship, service, fellowship with other Christians—these and more will become important parts of your walk with Him. The verses below, arranged under topical headings, would be good ones to look up and meditate on in the days ahead.

Again, welcome to the family of God! Remember that the Christian life is not about religion, rules, and regulations, but a relationship with Jesus Christ. Pursue Him as you would your dearest friend. Talk to Him, read His Word, invite Him to go with you and to guide you in every situation. And depend on His forgiveness when you fail.

Today really is the first day of the rest of your new life! May you sense God's love, and our love, as you begin your journey as a follower of Jesus.

1. SPEND TIME DAILY LISTENING TO GOD (BIBLE STUDY)

Deuteronomy 17:19　　　Proverbs 2:1–6
Joshua 1:8　　　　　　 Romans 10:17
Psalm 119:9, 11

2. SPEND TIME DAILY TALKING TO GOD (PRAYER)

Mathew 7:7–8　　　　 James 1:5
John 15:7　　　　　　 James 4:3
John 16:24　　　　　　1 Peter 5:7
Philippians 4:6–7　　　1 John 5:14–15

3. MEDITATE ON THE GRACE OF GOD (GRACE IS RECEIVING WHAT WE DON'T DESERVE)

John 1:14　　　　　　 Ephesians 2:8–9
Romans 8:1–2　　　　　Titus 2:11
1 Corinthians 1:4　　　 James 4:6

4. DEPEND ON GOD DAILY FOR GUIDANCE THROUGH THE HOLY SPIRIT

Psalm 32:8　　　　　　Romans 12:1–2
Proverbs 3:5–6　　　　 Ephesians 4:30
Jeremiah 29:13　　　　 Ephesians 5:18
John 15:5–17　　　　　1 Thessalonians 5:19
Romans 8

5. BELIEVE THAT GOD WILL NEVER LEAVE YOU AND IS AT WORK EVEN IN TIMES OF TROUBLE OR SORROW TO GIVE YOU VICTORY IN CHRIST.

Psalm 119:67, 71, 75　　Romans 5:3–5
Hebrews 13:5　　　　　Romans 8:28
1 Thessalonians 5:24　　2 Corinthians 12:7–10
Philippians 1:6　　　　 Hebrews 12:6-10
James 1:2–4

6. SURROUND YOURSELF WITH A GROUP OF LIKE-MINDED BELIEVERS IN CHRIST (A CHURCH HOME AND A BIBLE STUDY GROUP).

Math 28:18–20　　　　 2 Corinthians 5:17–20
Mark 3:14　　　　　　 Ephesians 1:22
Romans 12:5　　　　　 Ephesians 4:11–16